I CAN ...
AF256788 
SHOW KINDNESS
INSPIRE PEOPLE
BE A GOOD LISTENER
SET GOALS
LEARN FROM OTHERS
BELIEVE IN MYSELF
SET A GOOD EXAMPLE
HELP OTHERS
ADMIT MISTAKES
HELP PEOPLE
EMBRACE DIFFERENCES
BECAUSE I AM A LEADER
SIGNED,

DATE: S M T W TH F S __ / __ / __

OVERALL TODAY WAS: ☆ ☆ ☆ ☆ ☆

👍 TODAY'S TRIUMPHS

👎 TODAY'S CHALLENGES

💡 WHAT I LEARNED FROM TODAY:

🏆 MY TOP GOAL FOR TOMORROW:

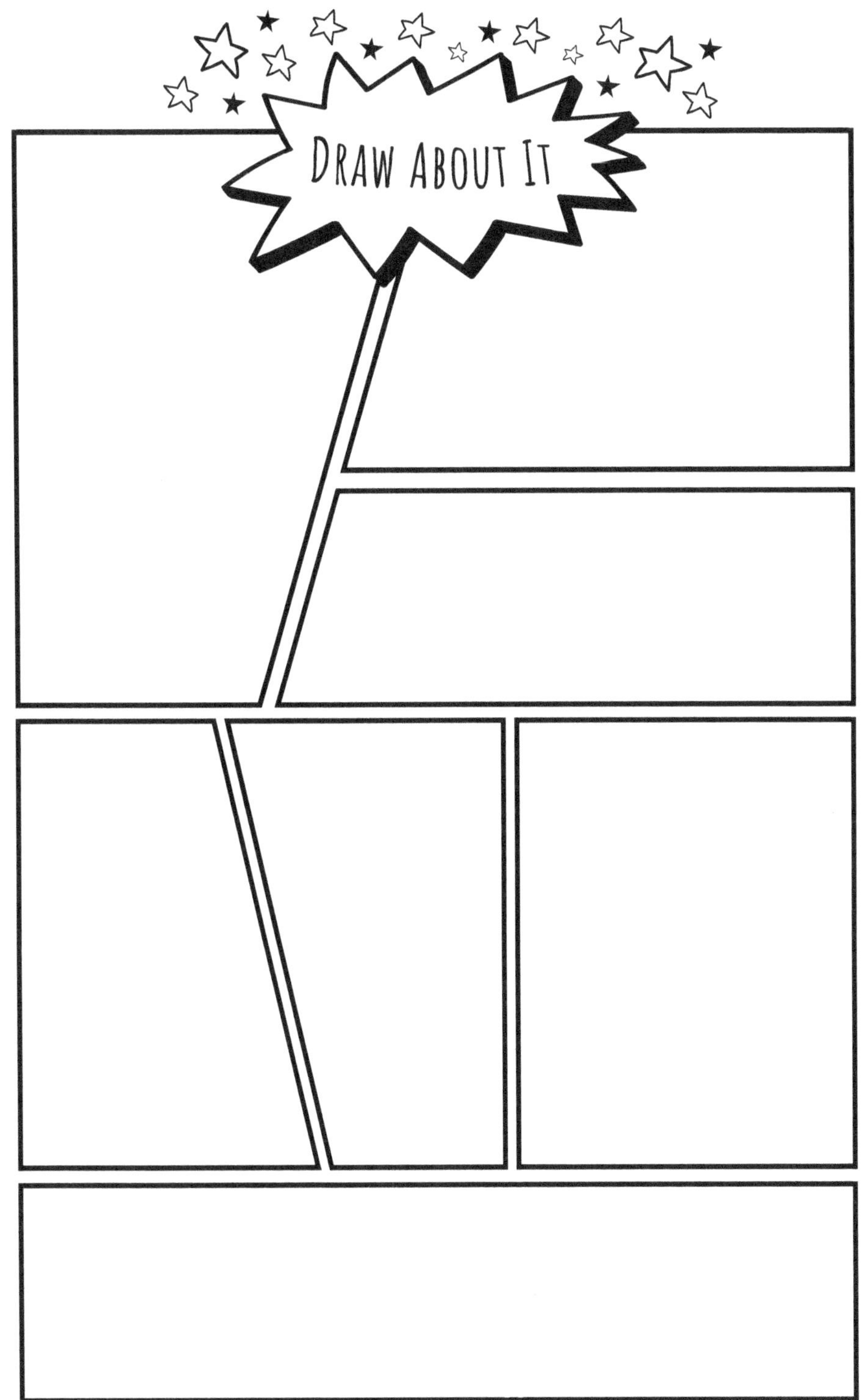
Draw About It

DATE: S M T W TH F S __ / __ / __

OVERALL TODAY WAS: ☆ ☆ ☆ ☆ ☆

👍 TODAY'S TRIUMPHS

👎 TODAY'S CHALLENGES

💡 WHAT I LEARNED FROM TODAY:

🏆 MY TOP GOAL FOR TOMORROW:

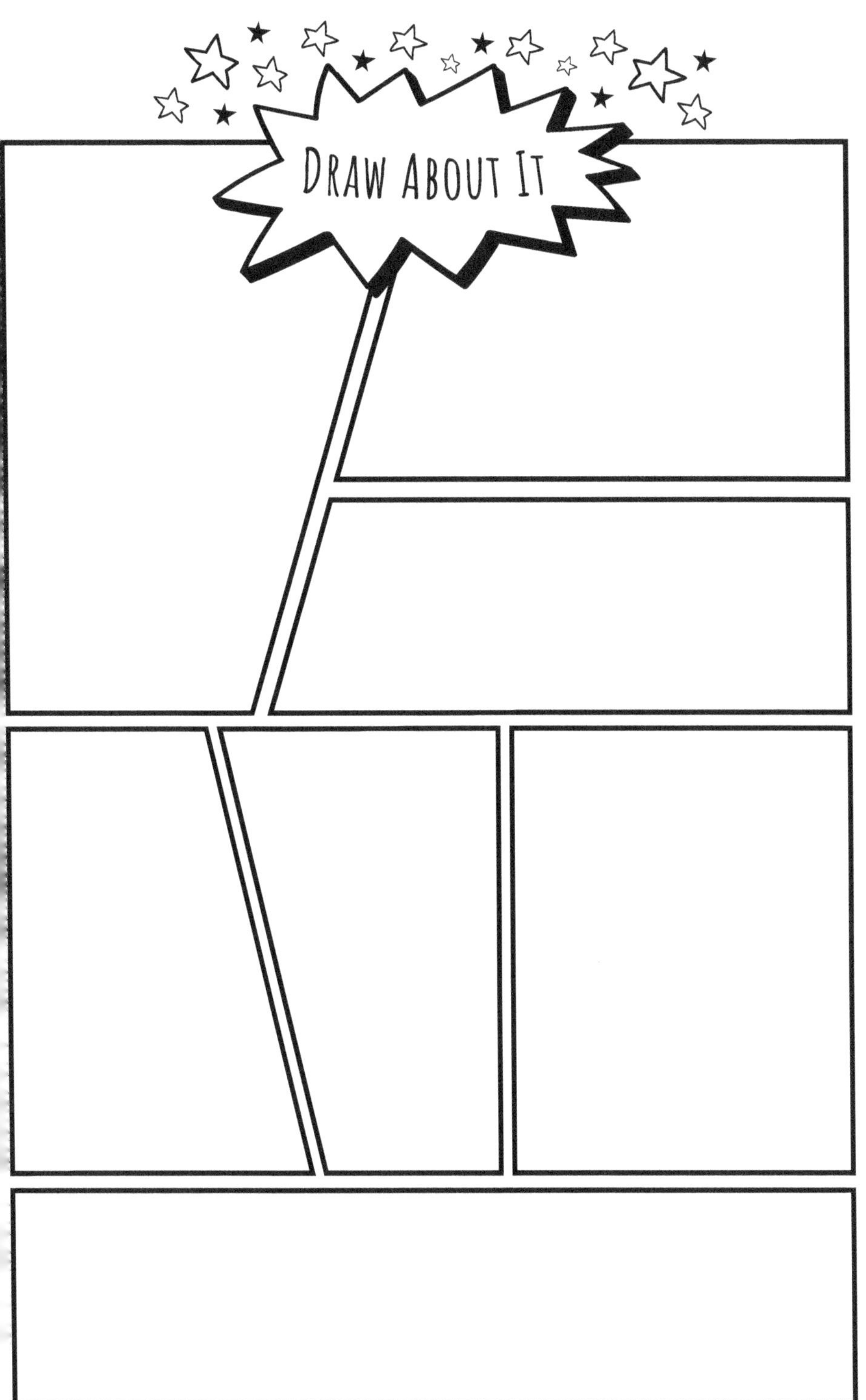
Draw About It

DATE: S M T W TH F S __ / __ / __

OVERALL TODAY WAS:

👍 TODAY'S TRIUMPHS

👎 TODAY'S CHALLENGES

💡 WHAT I LEARNED FROM TODAY:

🏆 MY TOP GOAL FOR TOMORROW:

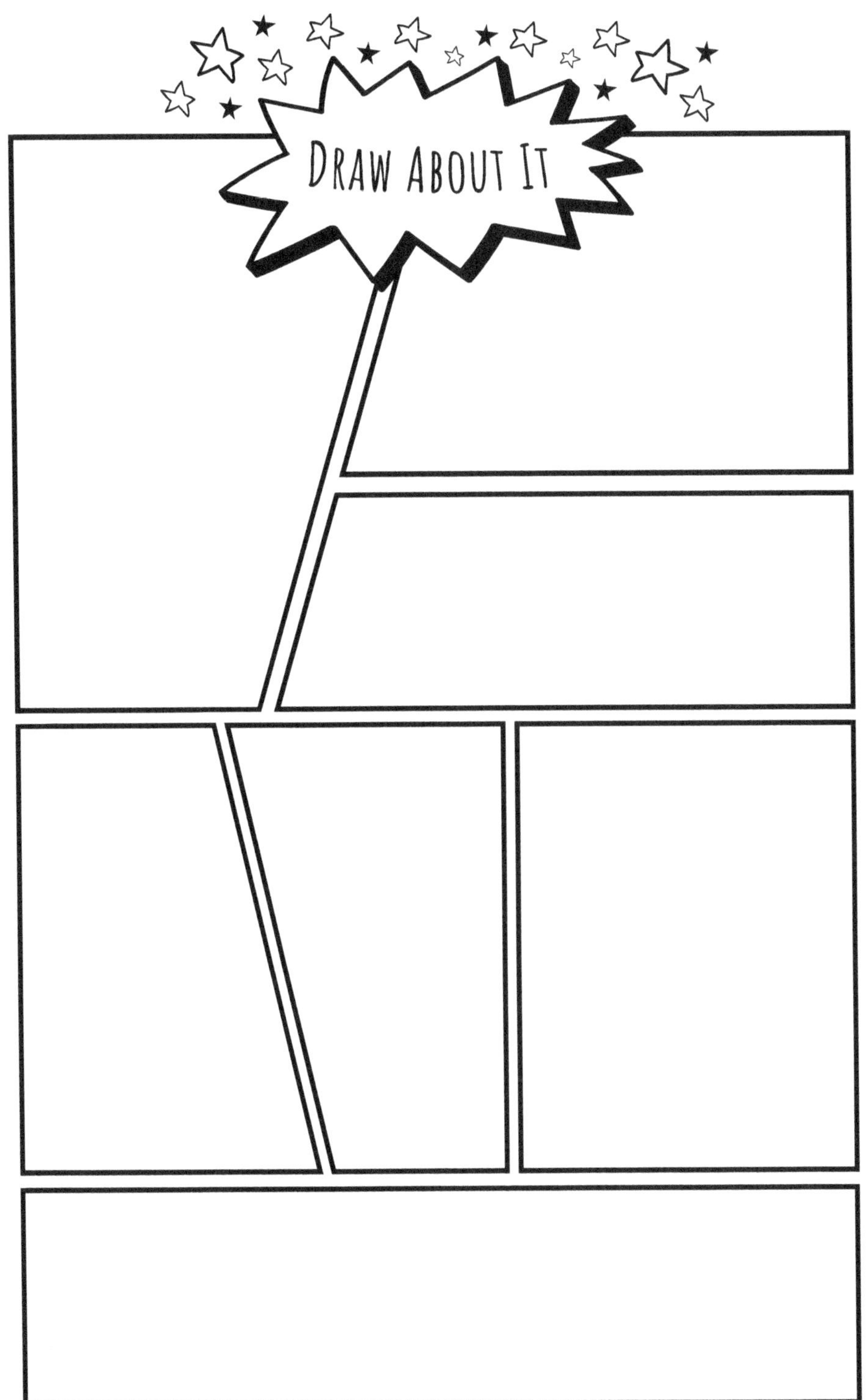
DRAW ABOUT IT

DATE: S M T W TH F S __ / __ / __

OVERALL TODAY WAS: ☆ ☆ ☆ ☆ ☆

👍 TODAY'S TRIUMPHS

👎 TODAY'S CHALLENGES

💡 WHAT I LEARNED FROM TODAY:

🏆 MY TOP GOAL FOR TOMORROW:

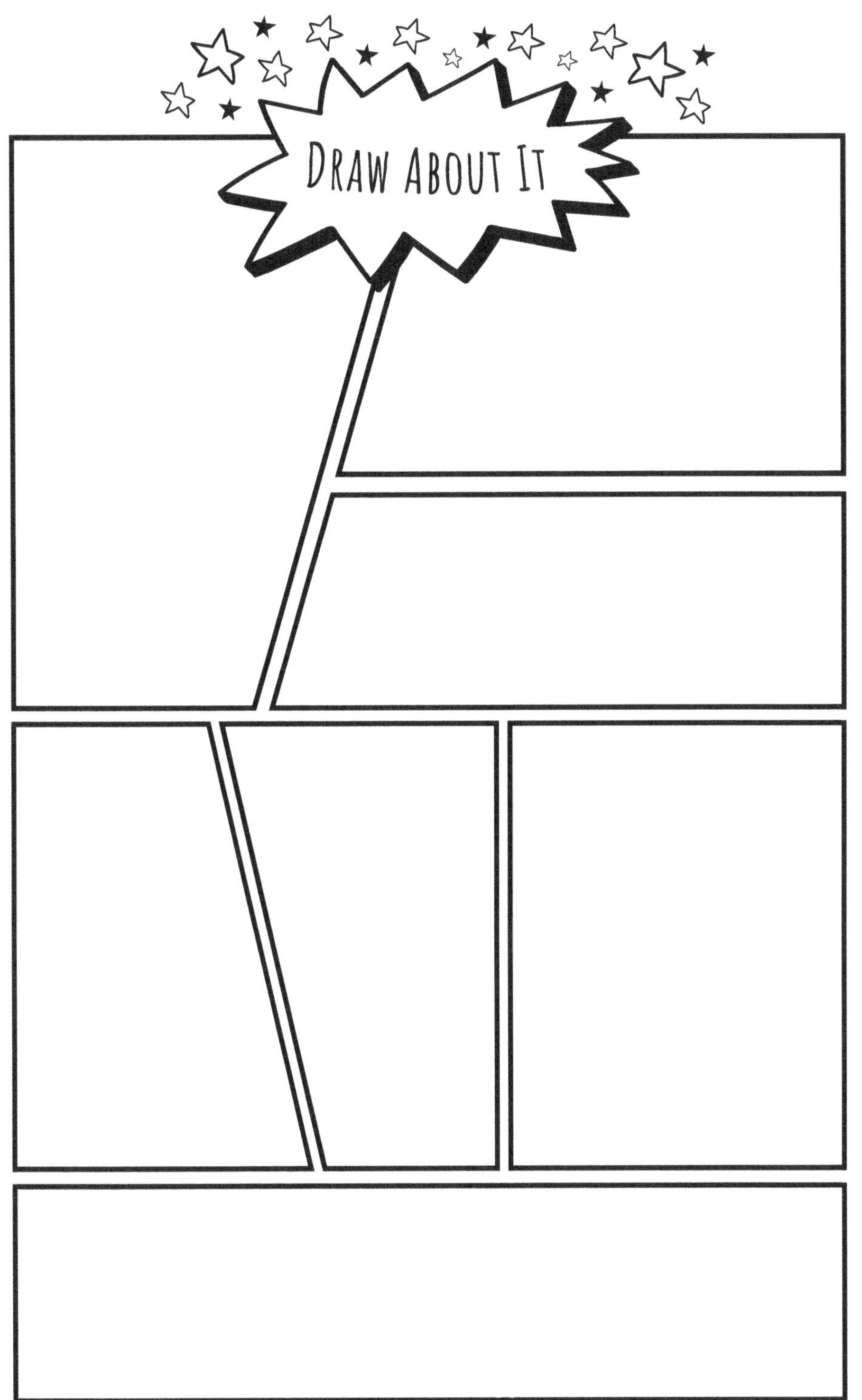

DRAW ABOUT IT

DATE: S M T W TH F S __ / __ / __

OVERALL TODAY WAS: ☆ ☆ ☆ ☆ ☆

👍 TODAY'S TRIUMPHS

👎 TODAY'S CHALLENGES

💡 WHAT I LEARNED FROM TODAY:

🏆 MY TOP GOAL FOR TOMORROW:

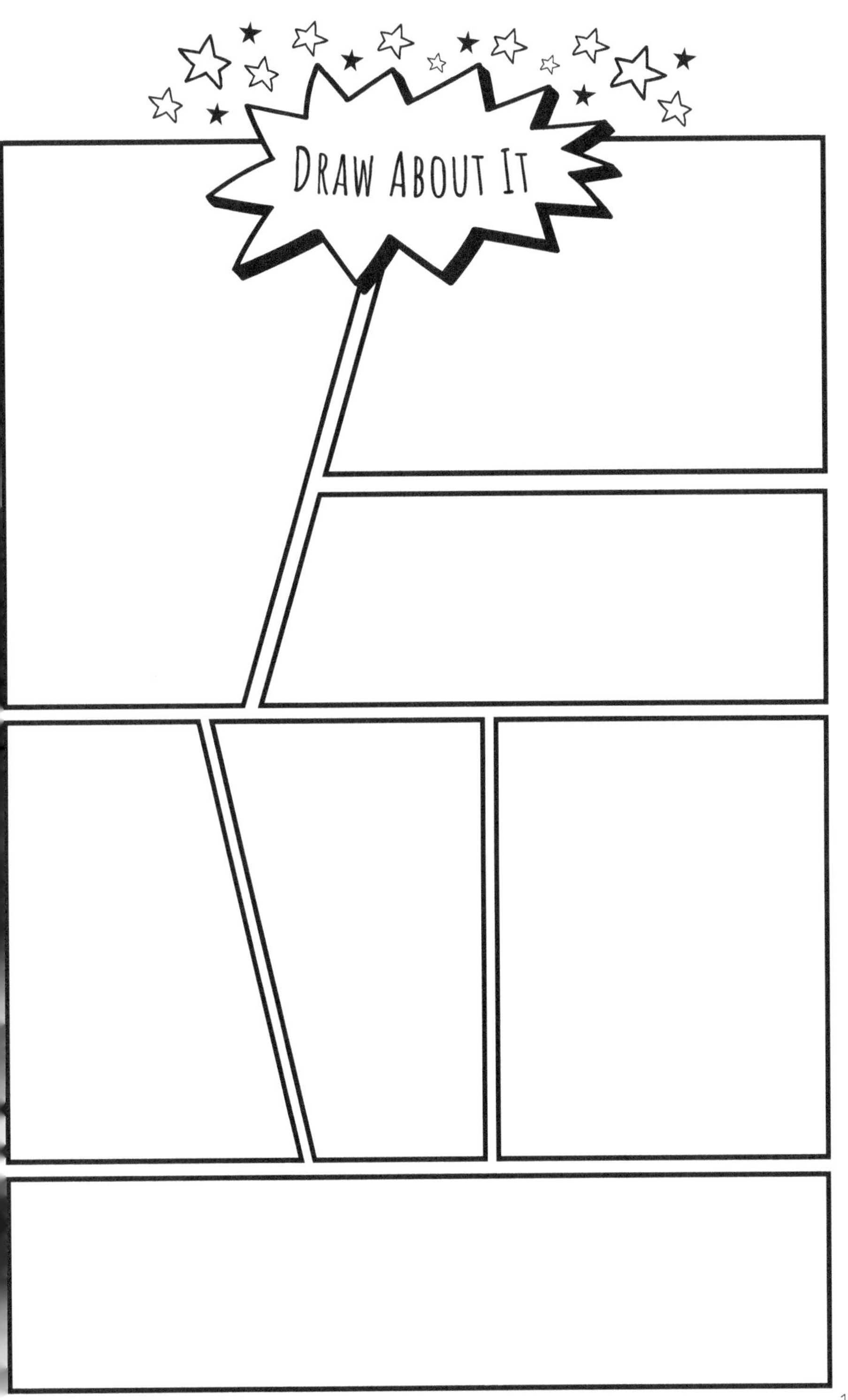
DRAW ABOUT IT

DATE: S M T W TH F S __ / __ / __

OVERALL TODAY WAS: ☆ ☆ ☆ ☆ ☆

👍 TODAY'S TRIUMPHS

👎 TODAY'S CHALLENGES

💡 WHAT I LEARNED FROM TODAY:

🏆 MY TOP GOAL FOR TOMORROW:

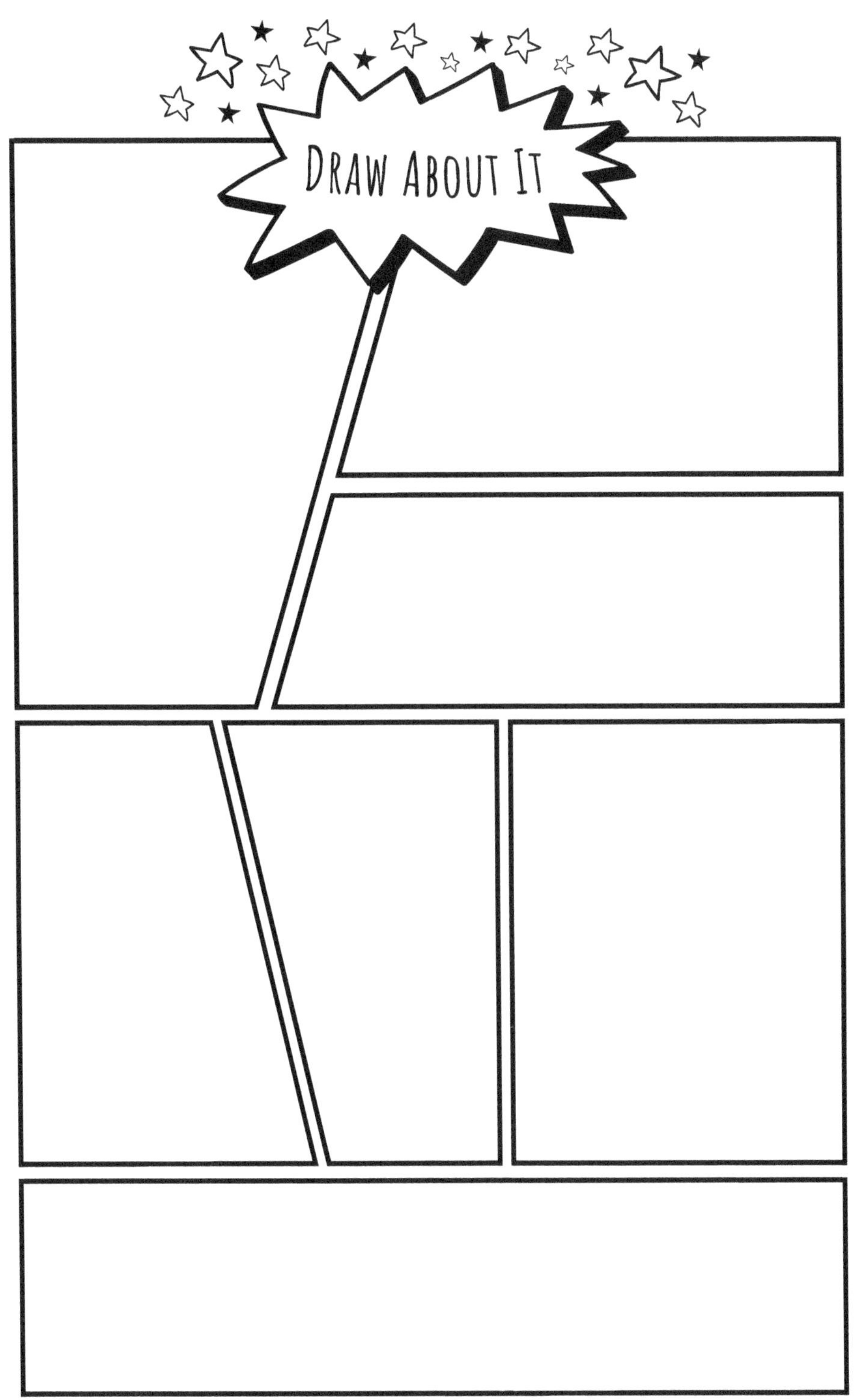
DRAW ABOUT IT

DATE: S M T W TH F S __ / __ / __

OVERALL TODAY WAS: ☆ ☆ ☆ ☆ ☆

👍 TODAY'S TRIUMPHS

👎 TODAY'S CHALLENGES

 WHAT I LEARNED FROM TODAY:

 MY TOP GOAL FOR TOMORROW:

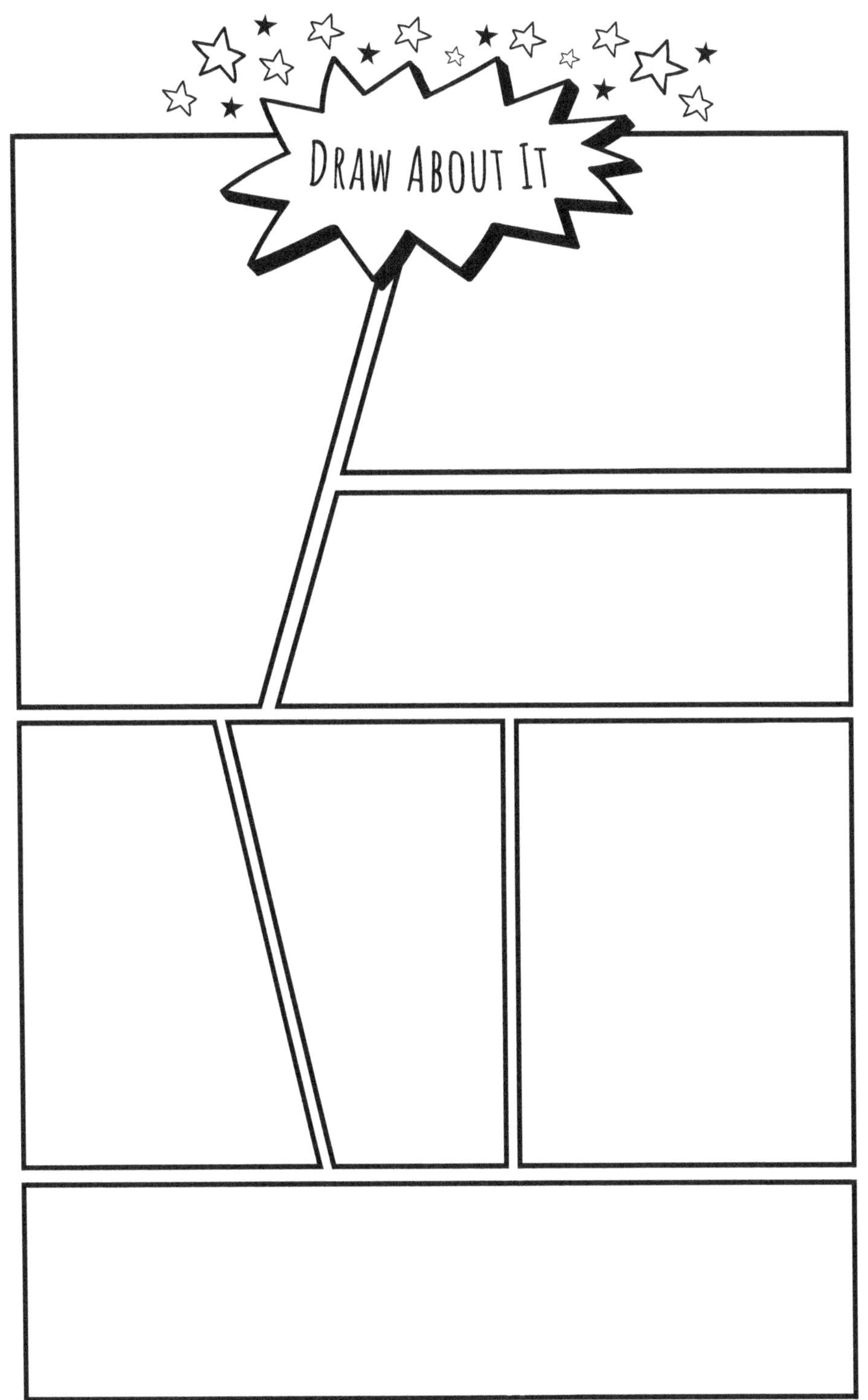
Draw About It

DATE: S M T W TH F S   __ / __ / __

OVERALL TODAY WAS: ☆ ☆ ☆ ☆ ☆

👍 TODAY'S TRIUMPHS

👎 TODAY'S CHALLENGES

💡 WHAT I LEARNED FROM TODAY:

🏆 MY TOP GOAL FOR TOMORROW:

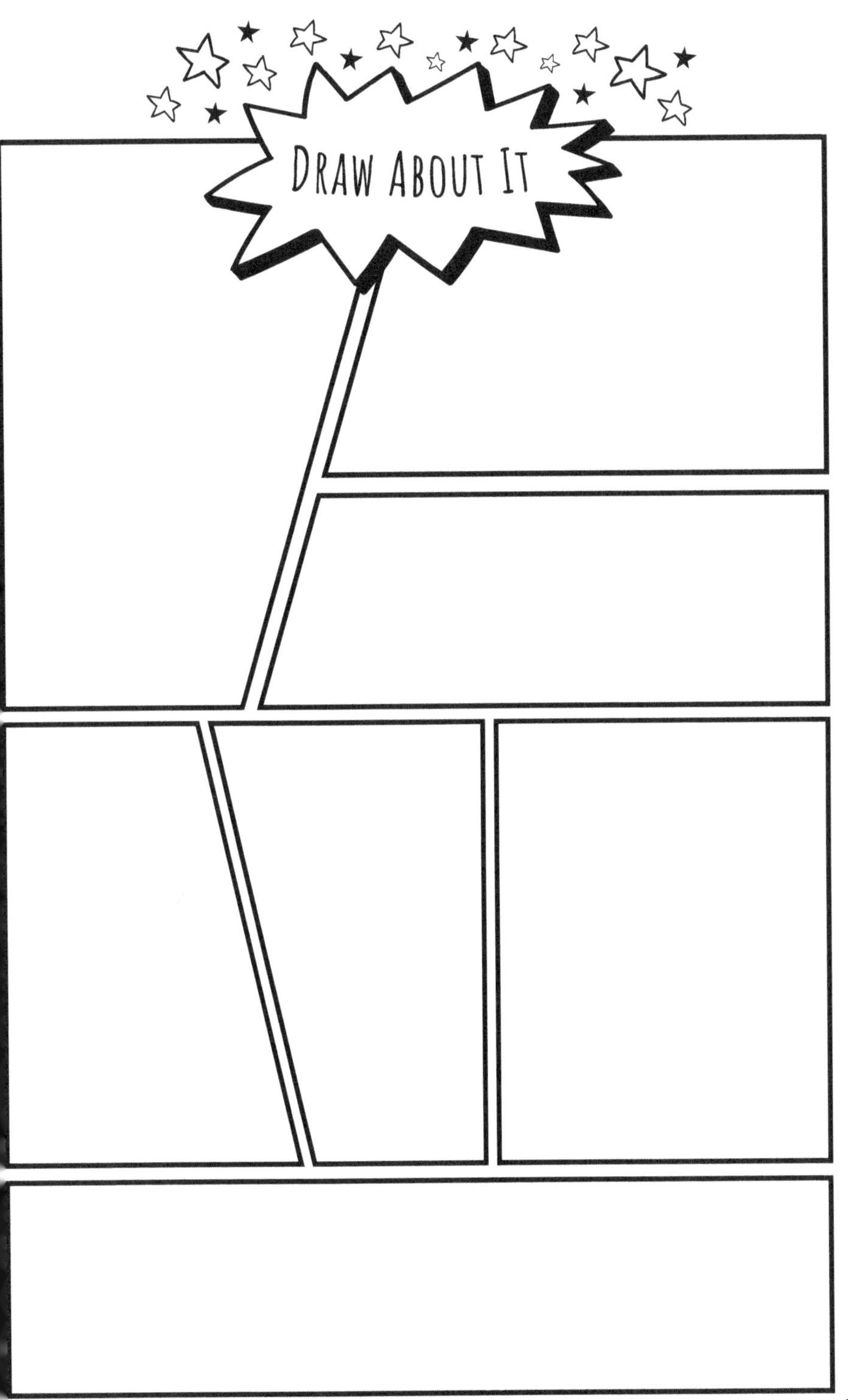

DRAW ABOUT IT

DATE: S M T W TH F S   __ / __ / __

OVERALL TODAY WAS: ☆ ☆ ☆ ☆ ☆

👍 TODAY'S TRIUMPHS

👎 TODAY'S CHALLENGES

💡 WHAT I LEARNED FROM TODAY:

🏆 MY TOP GOAL FOR TOMORROW:

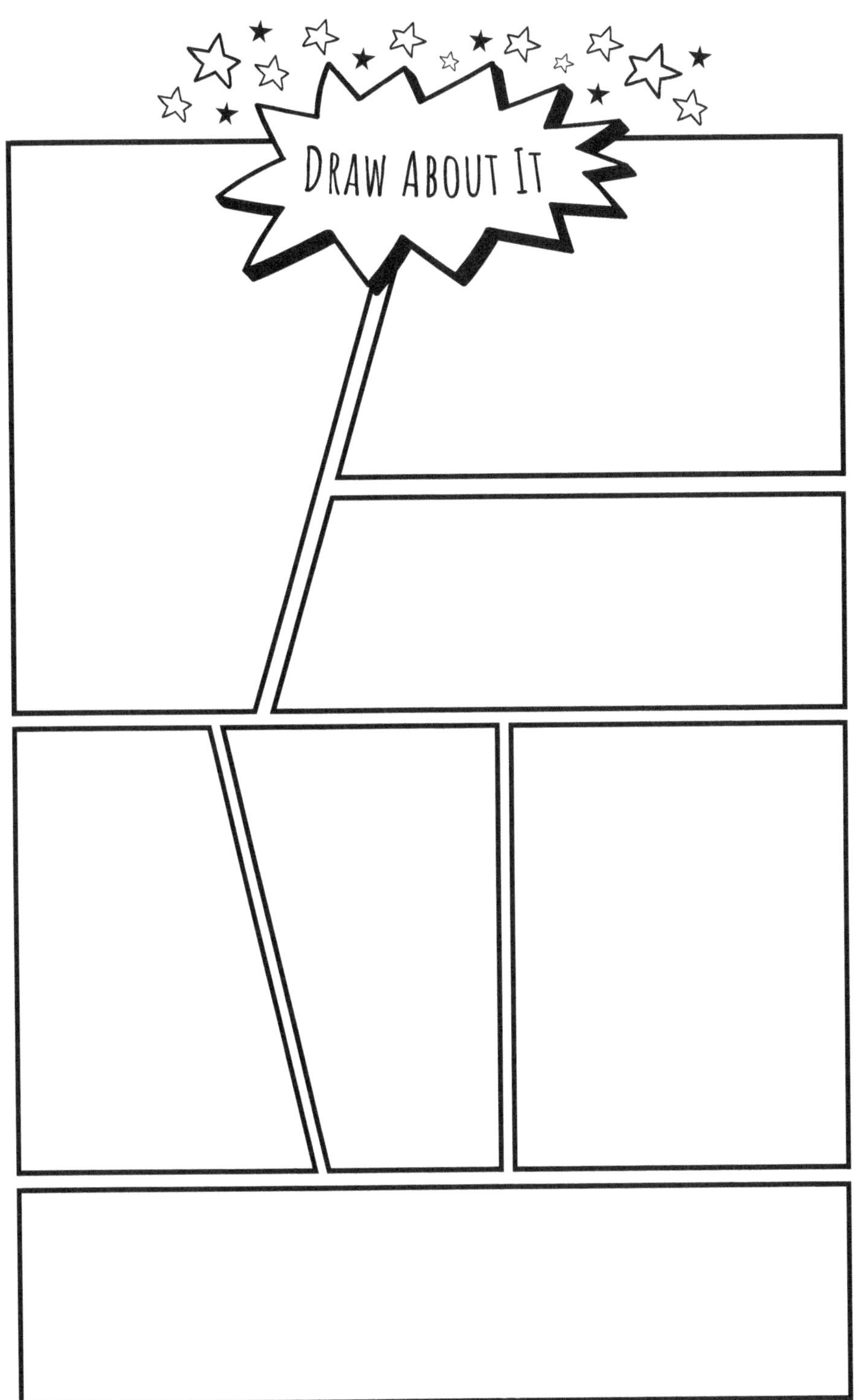
Draw About It

DATE: S M T W TH F S __ / __ / __

OVERALL TODAY WAS: ☆ ☆ ☆ ☆ ☆

👍 TODAY'S TRIUMPHS

____
____
____
____
____
____
____
____
____
____

👎 TODAY'S CHALLENGES

____
____
____
____
____
____
____
____
____

 WHAT I LEARNED FROM TODAY:

____
____

🏆 MY TOP GOAL FOR TOMORROW:

____

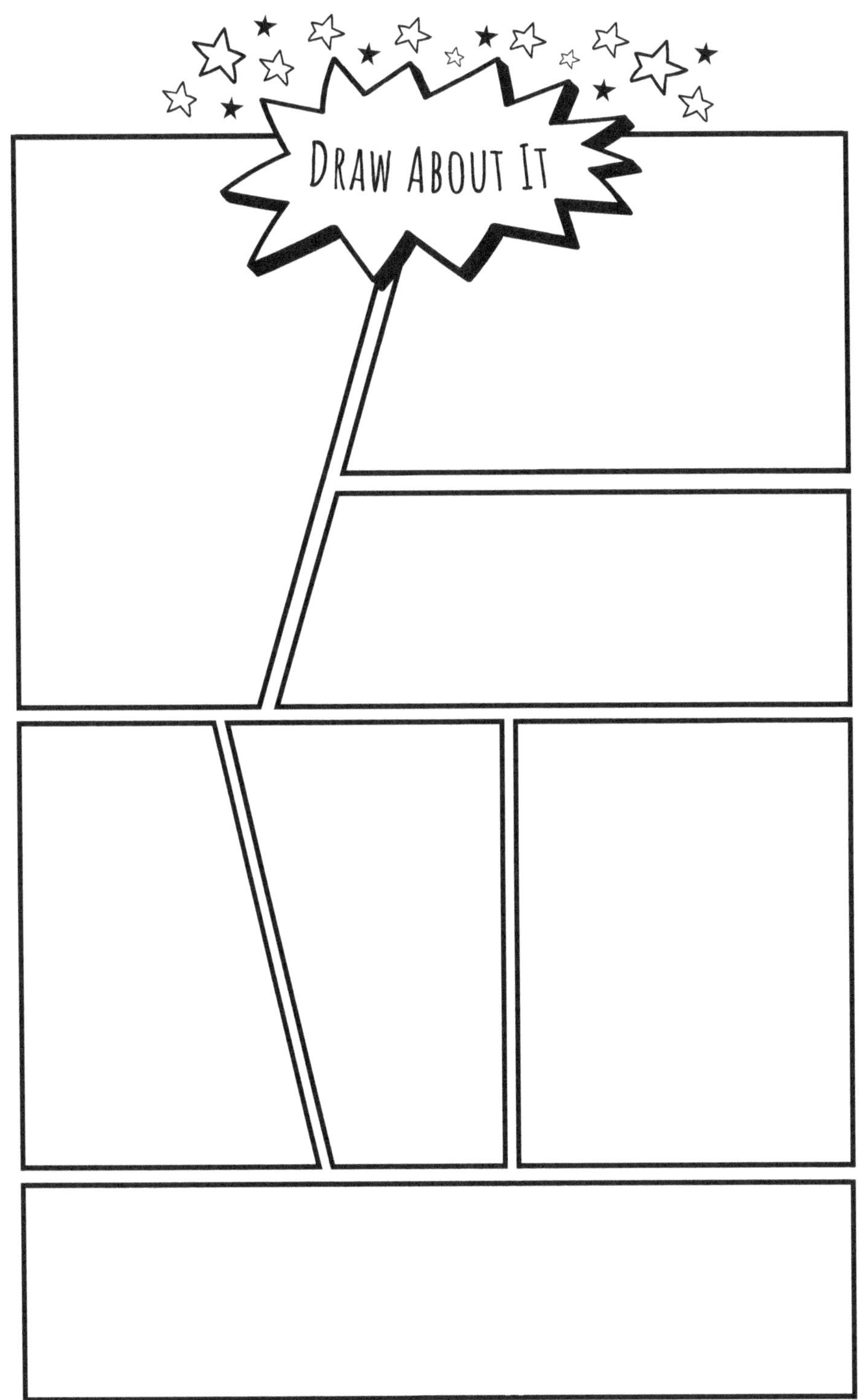
Draw About It

DATE: S M T W TH F S __ / __ / __

OVERALL TODAY WAS: ☆ ☆ ☆ ☆ ☆

👍 TODAY'S TRIUMPHS

👎 TODAY'S CHALLENGES

💡 WHAT I LEARNED FROM TODAY:

🏆 MY TOP GOAL FOR TOMORROW:

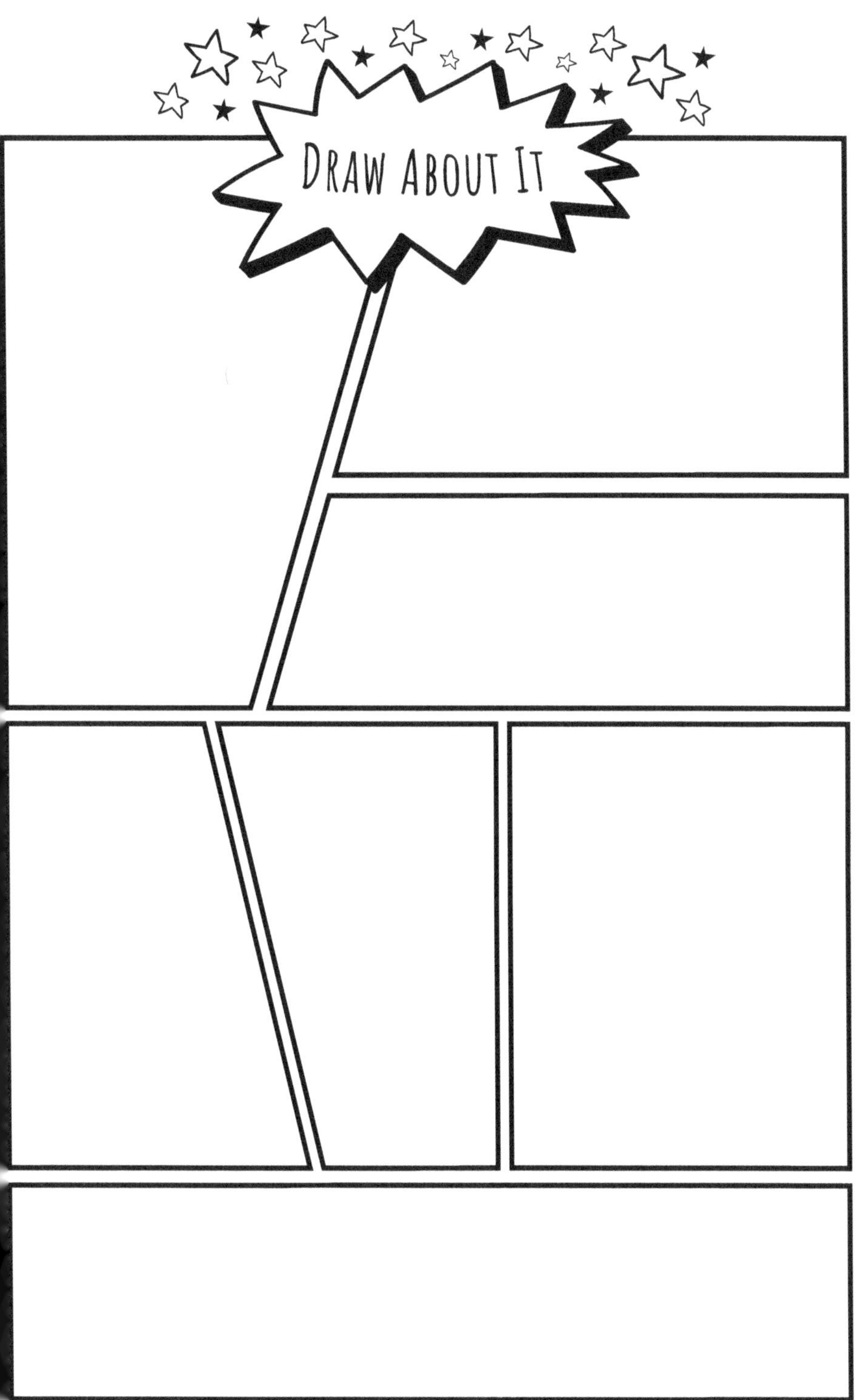
Draw About It

DATE: S M T W TH F S   __ / __ / __

OVERALL TODAY WAS: ☆ ☆ ☆ ☆ ☆

👍 TODAY'S TRIUMPHS

👎 TODAY'S CHALLENGES

💡 WHAT I LEARNED FROM TODAY:

🏆 MY TOP GOAL FOR TOMORROW:

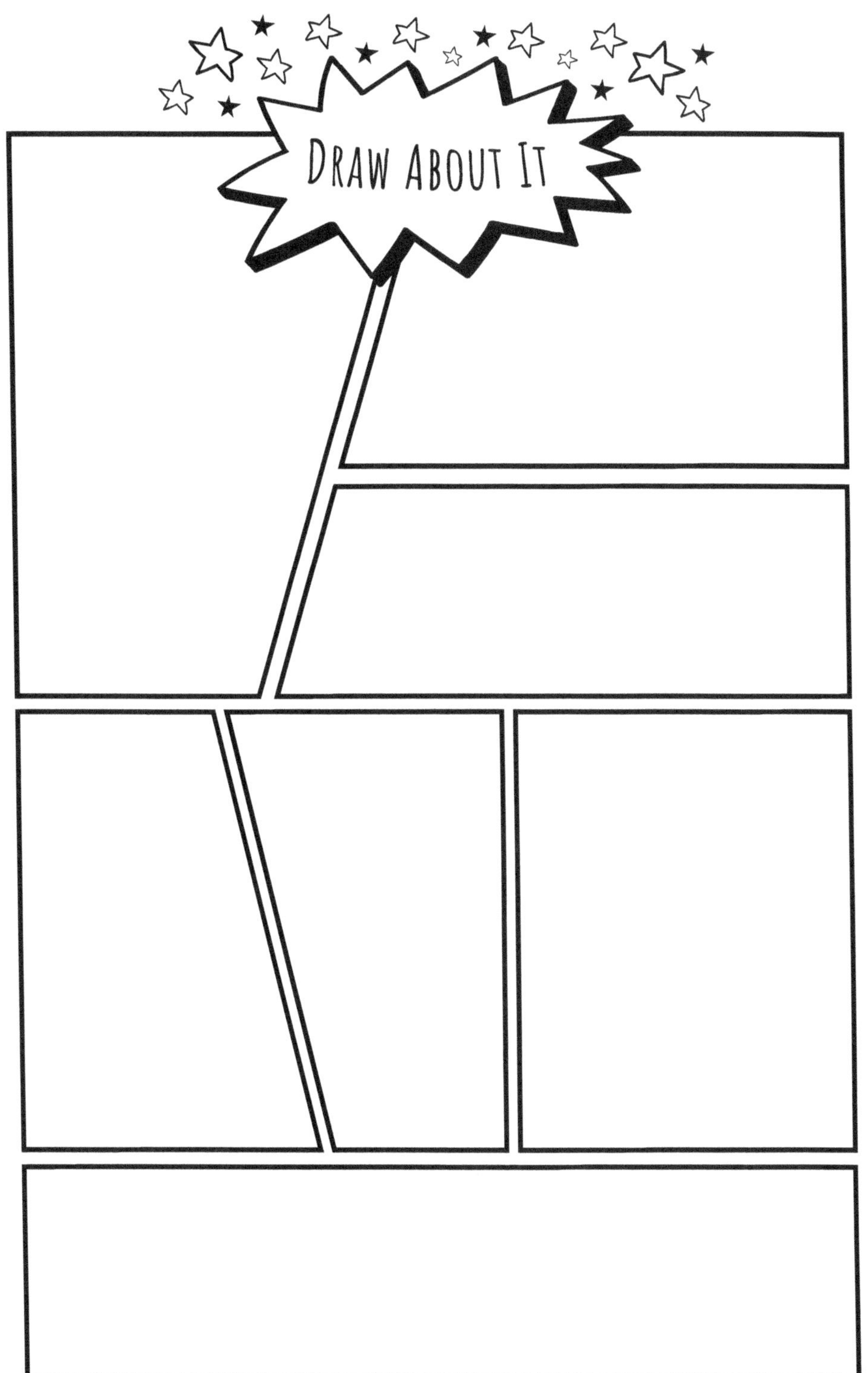
Draw About It

DATE: S M T W TH F S   __ / __ / __

OVERALL TODAY WAS: ☆ ☆ ☆ ☆ ☆

👍 TODAY'S TRIUMPHS

👎 TODAY'S CHALLENGES

💡 WHAT I LEARNED FROM TODAY:

🏆 MY TOP GOAL FOR TOMORROW:

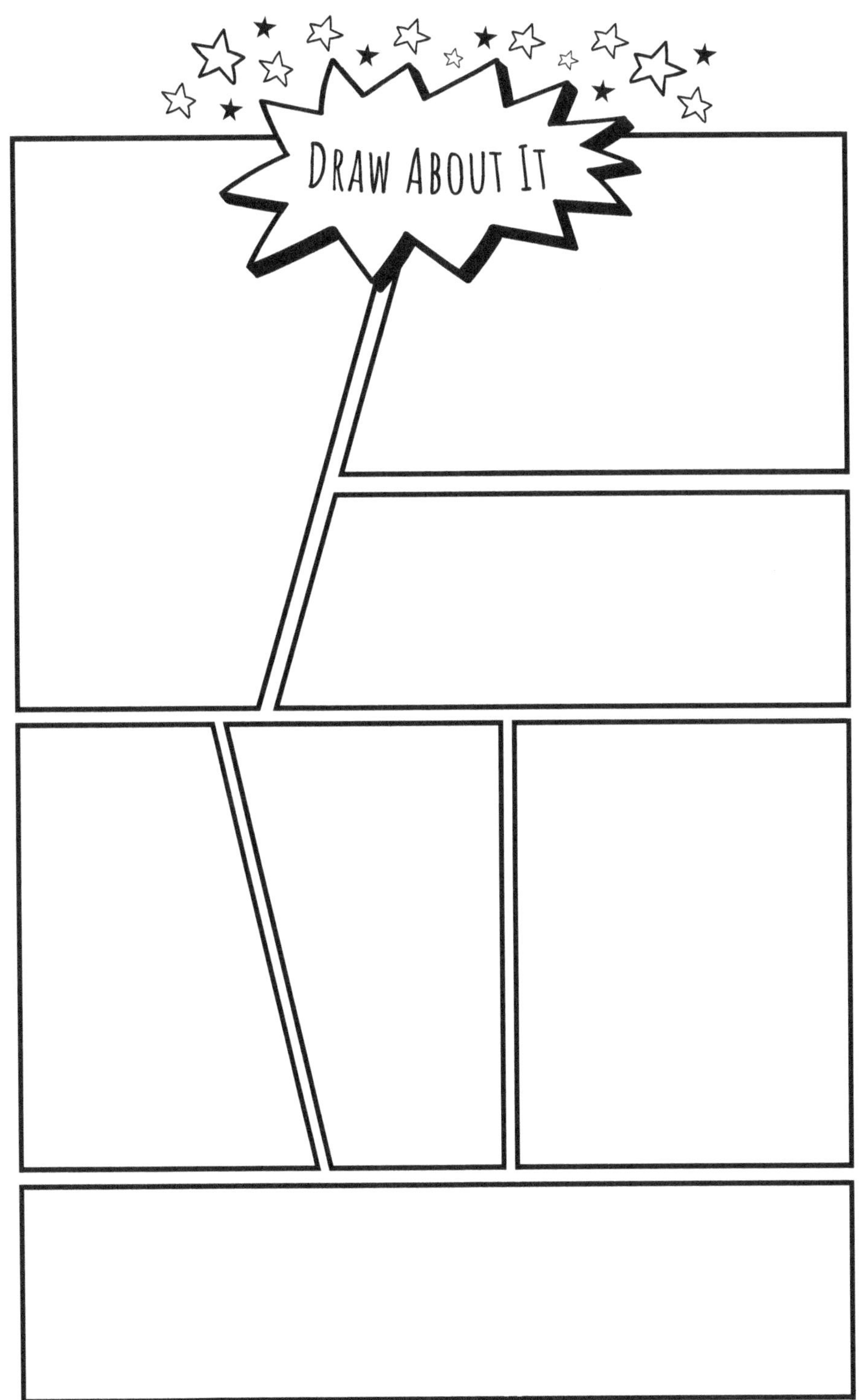
Draw About It

DATE: S M T W TH F S __ / __ / __

OVERALL TODAY WAS: ☆ ☆ ☆ ☆ ☆

👍 TODAY'S TRIUMPHS

👎 TODAY'S CHALLENGES

💡 WHAT I LEARNED FROM TODAY:

🏆 MY TOP GOAL FOR TOMORROW:

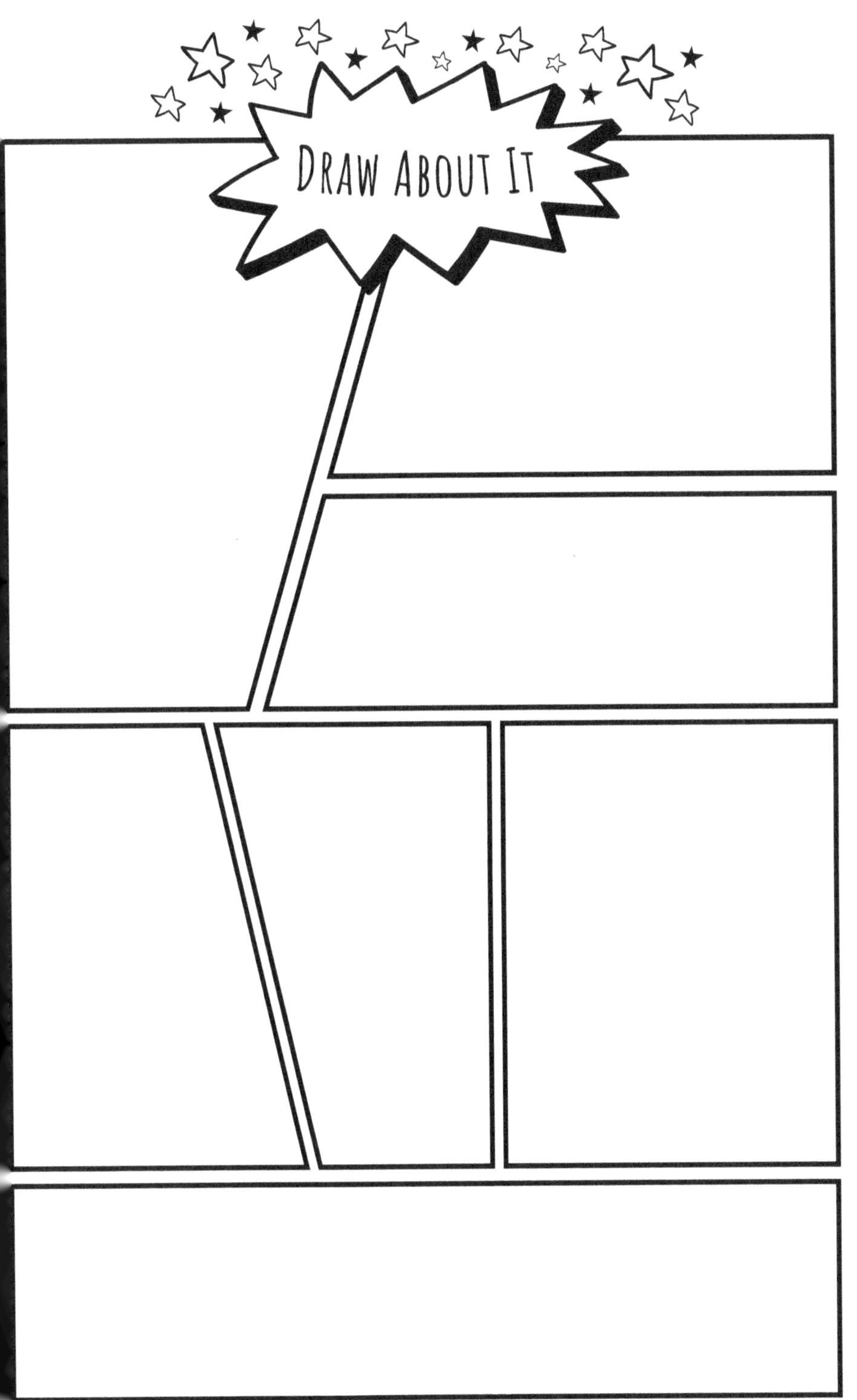
DRAW ABOUT IT

DATE: S M T W TH F S   __ / __ / __

OVERALL TODAY WAS: ☆ ☆ ☆ ☆ ☆

👍 TODAY'S TRIUMPHS

👎 TODAY'S CHALLENGES

💡 WHAT I LEARNED FROM TODAY:

🏆 MY TOP GOAL FOR TOMORROW:

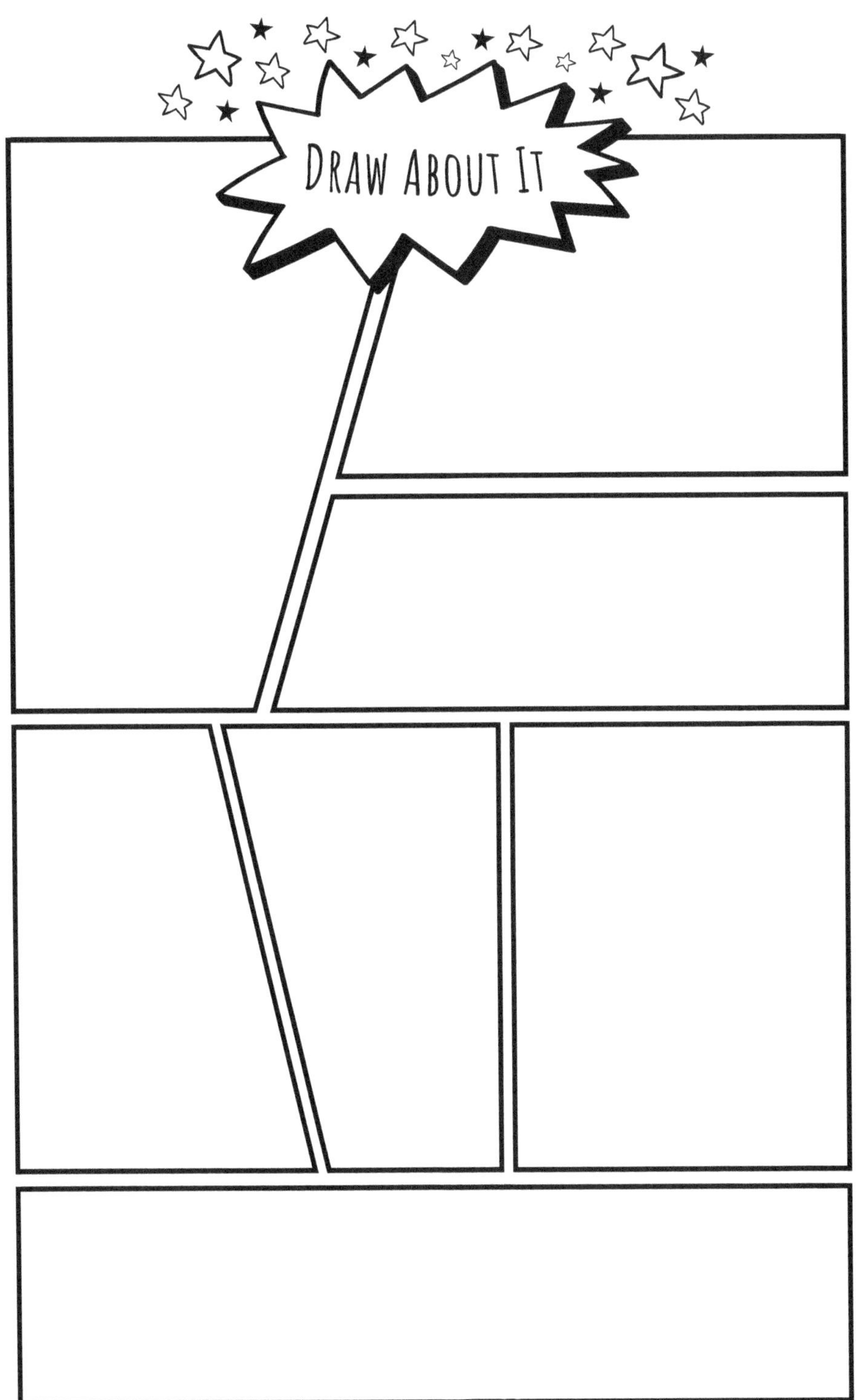
Draw About It

DATE: S M T W TH F S __ / __ / __

OVERALL TODAY WAS: ☆ ☆ ☆ ☆ ☆

👍 TODAY'S TRIUMPHS

👎 TODAY'S CHALLENGES

💡 WHAT I LEARNED FROM TODAY:

🏆 MY TOP GOAL FOR TOMORROW:

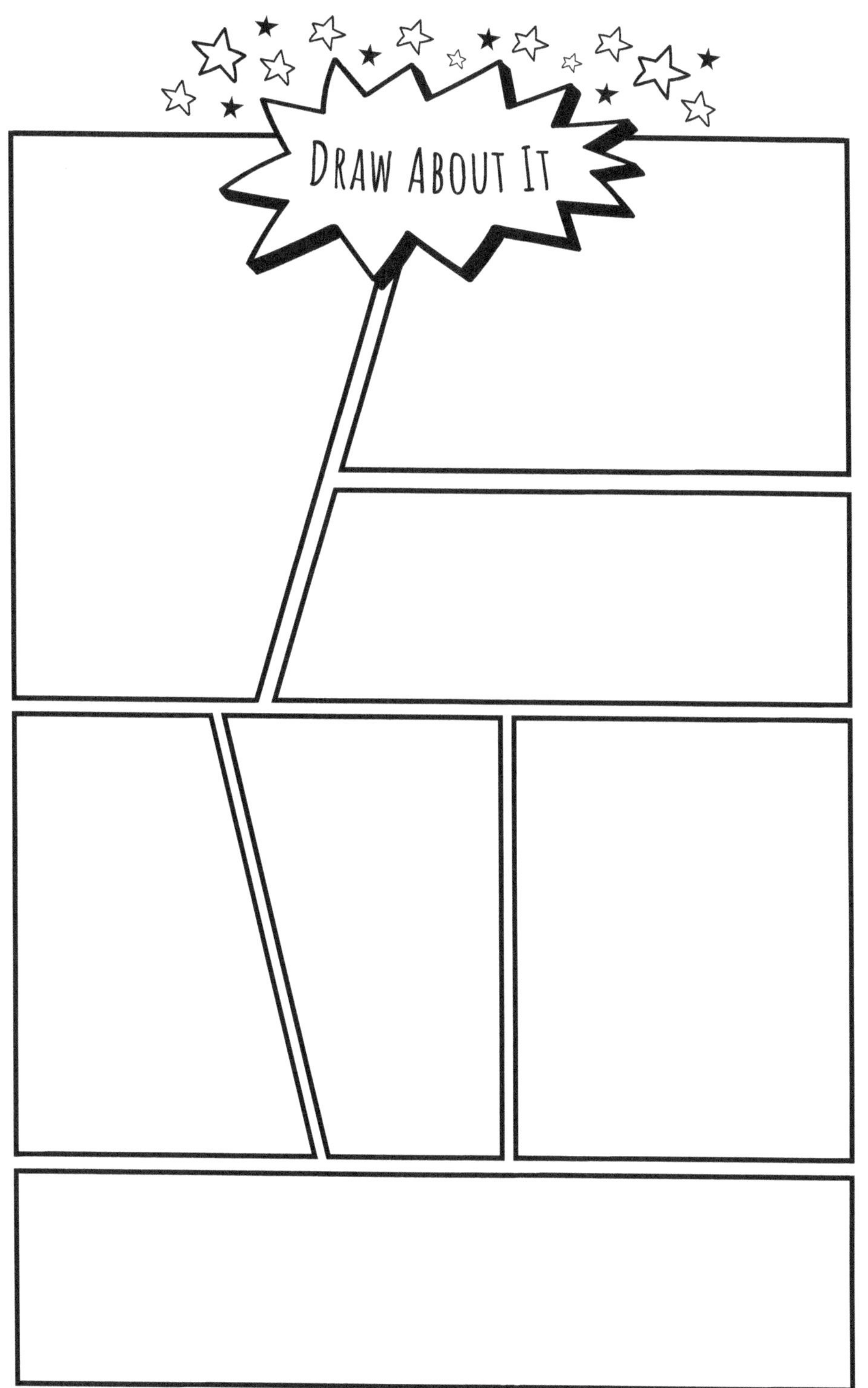
Draw About It

DATE: S M T W TH F S __ / __ / __

OVERALL TODAY WAS: ☆ ☆ ☆ ☆ ☆

👍 TODAY'S TRIUMPHS

👎 TODAY'S CHALLENGES

💡 WHAT I LEARNED FROM TODAY:

🏆 MY TOP GOAL FOR TOMORROW:

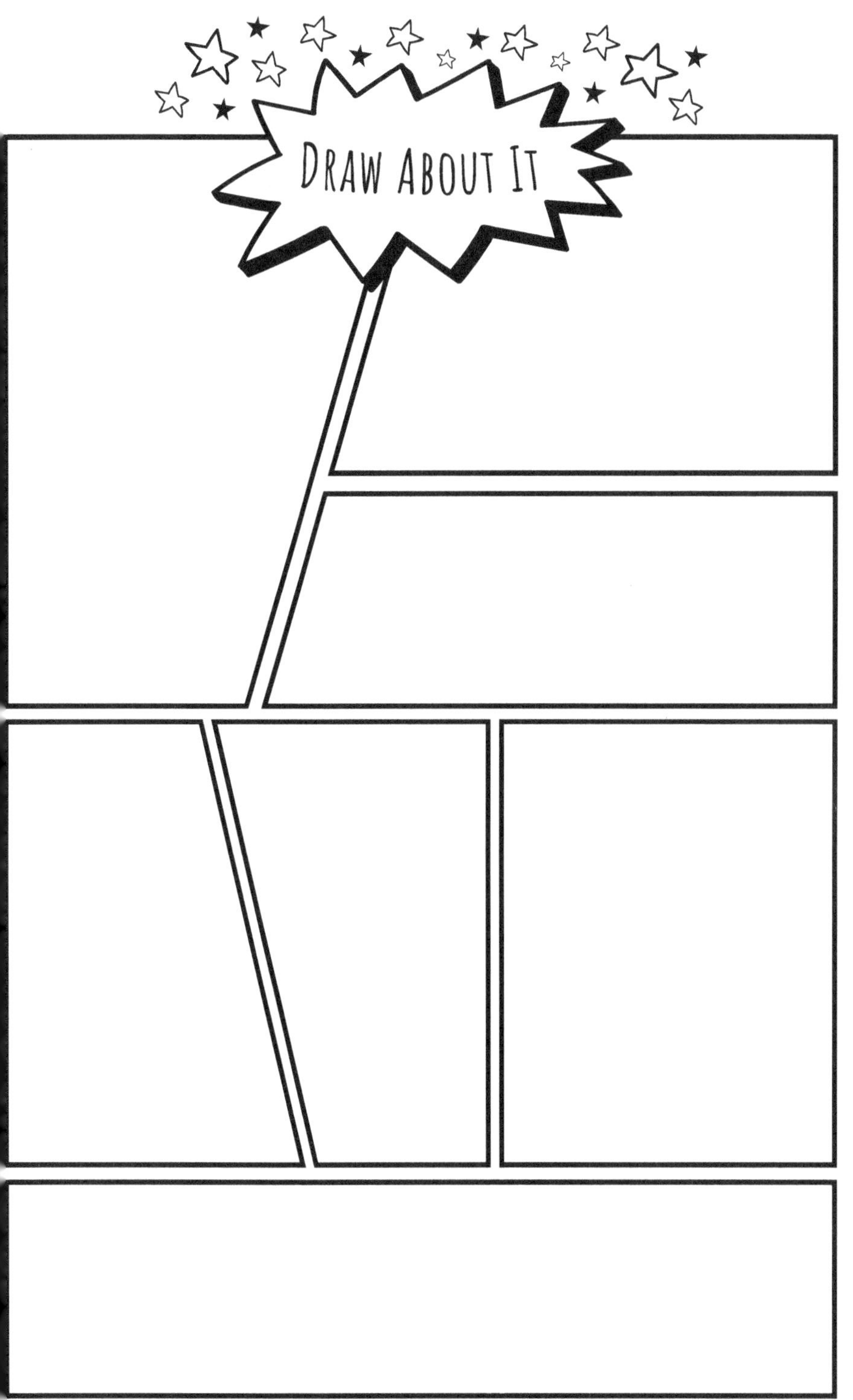

Draw About It

DATE: S M T W TH F S ___/___/___

OVERALL TODAY WAS: ☆ ☆ ☆ ☆ ☆

👍 TODAY'S TRIUMPHS

👎 TODAY'S CHALLENGES

💡 WHAT I LEARNED FROM TODAY:

🏆 MY TOP GOAL FOR TOMORROW:

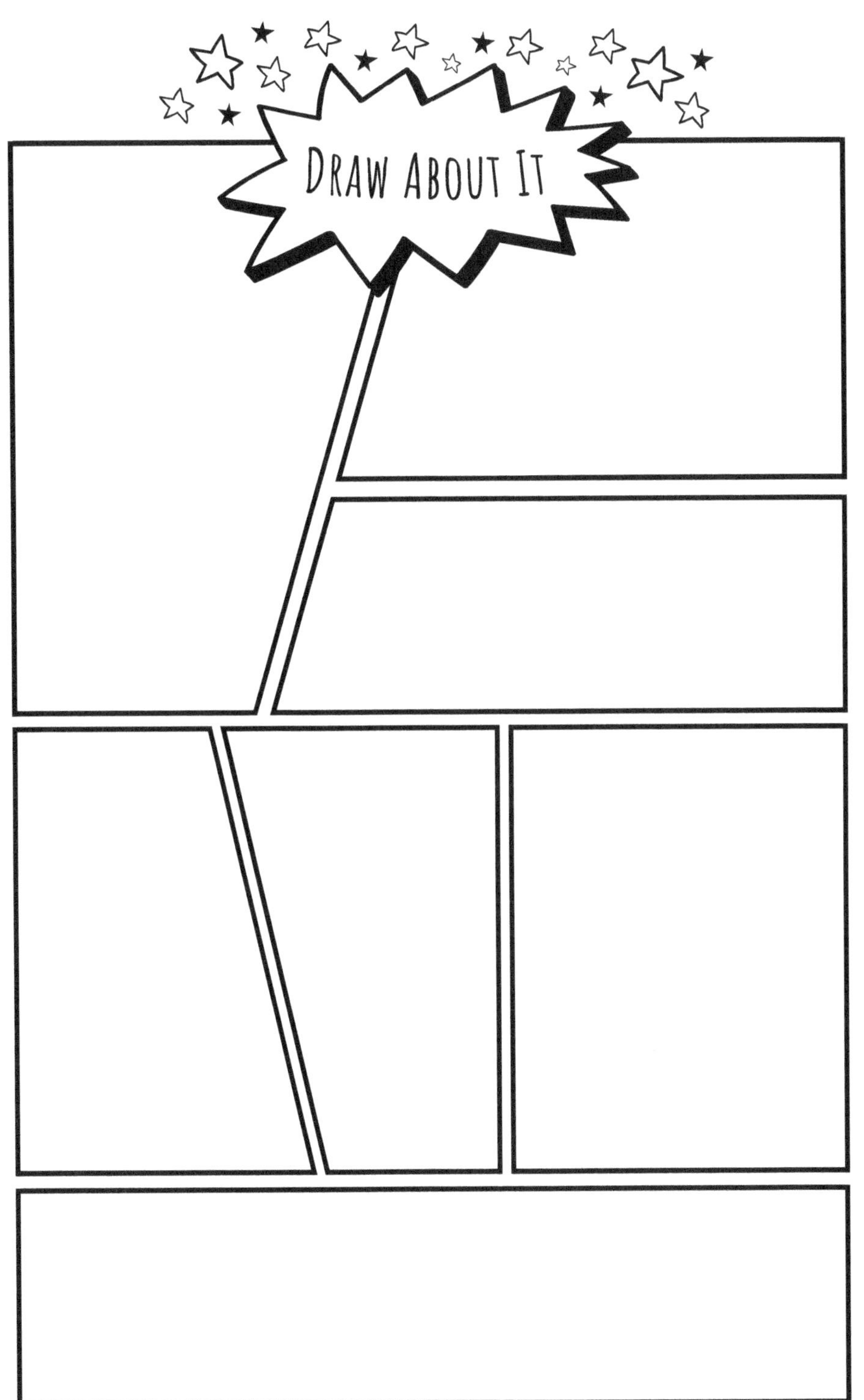

Draw About It

DATE: S M T W TH F S __ / __ / __

OVERALL TODAY WAS: ☆ ☆ ☆ ☆ ☆

👍 TODAY'S TRIUMPHS

👎 TODAY'S CHALLENGES

💡 WHAT I LEARNED FROM TODAY:

🏆 MY TOP GOAL FOR TOMORROW:

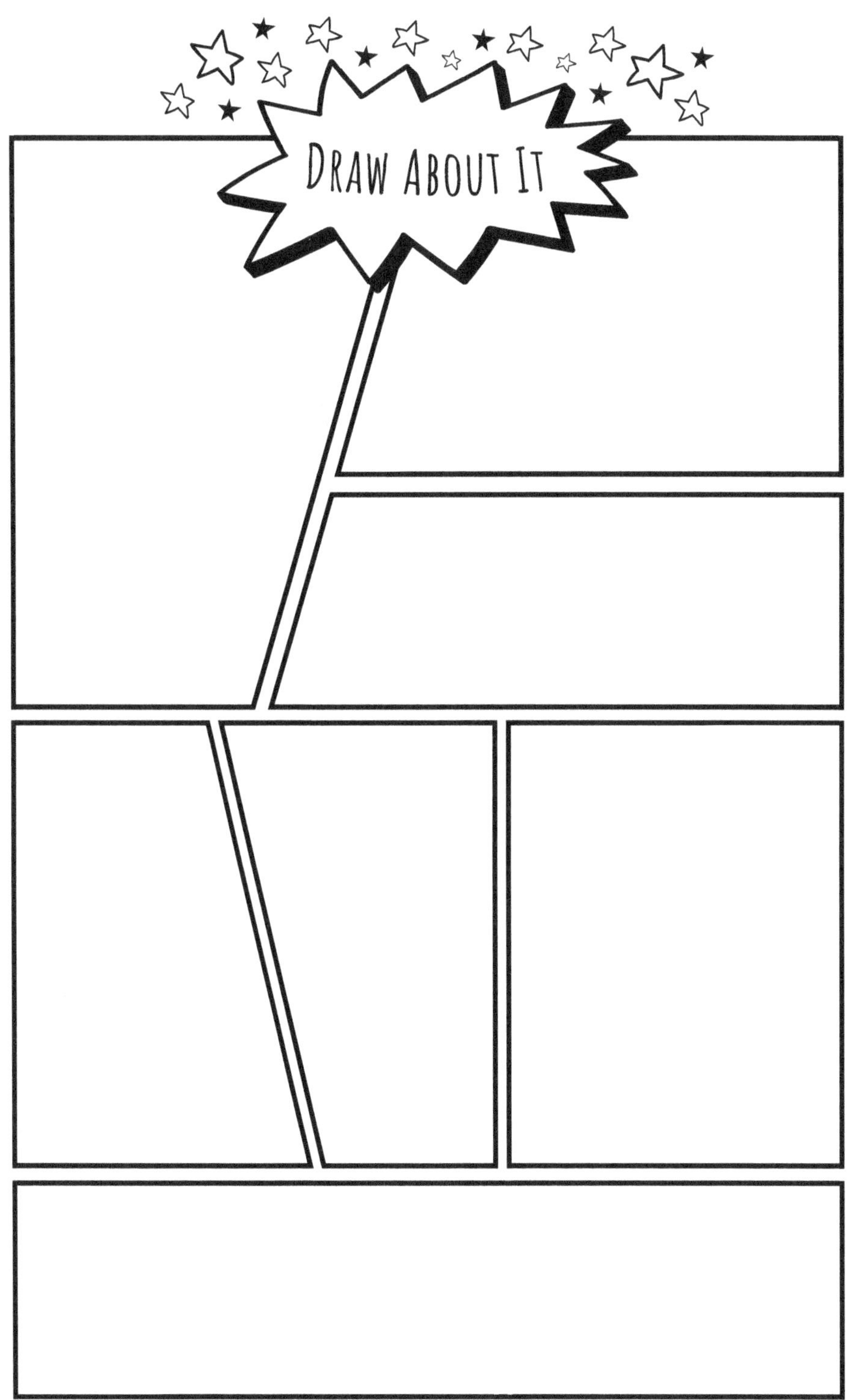

Draw About It

DATE: S M T W TH F S __ / __ / __

OVERALL TODAY WAS: ☆ ☆ ☆ ☆ ☆

👍 TODAY'S TRIUMPHS

👎 TODAY'S CHALLENGES

★

💡 WHAT I LEARNED FROM TODAY:

🏆 MY TOP GOAL FOR TOMORROW:

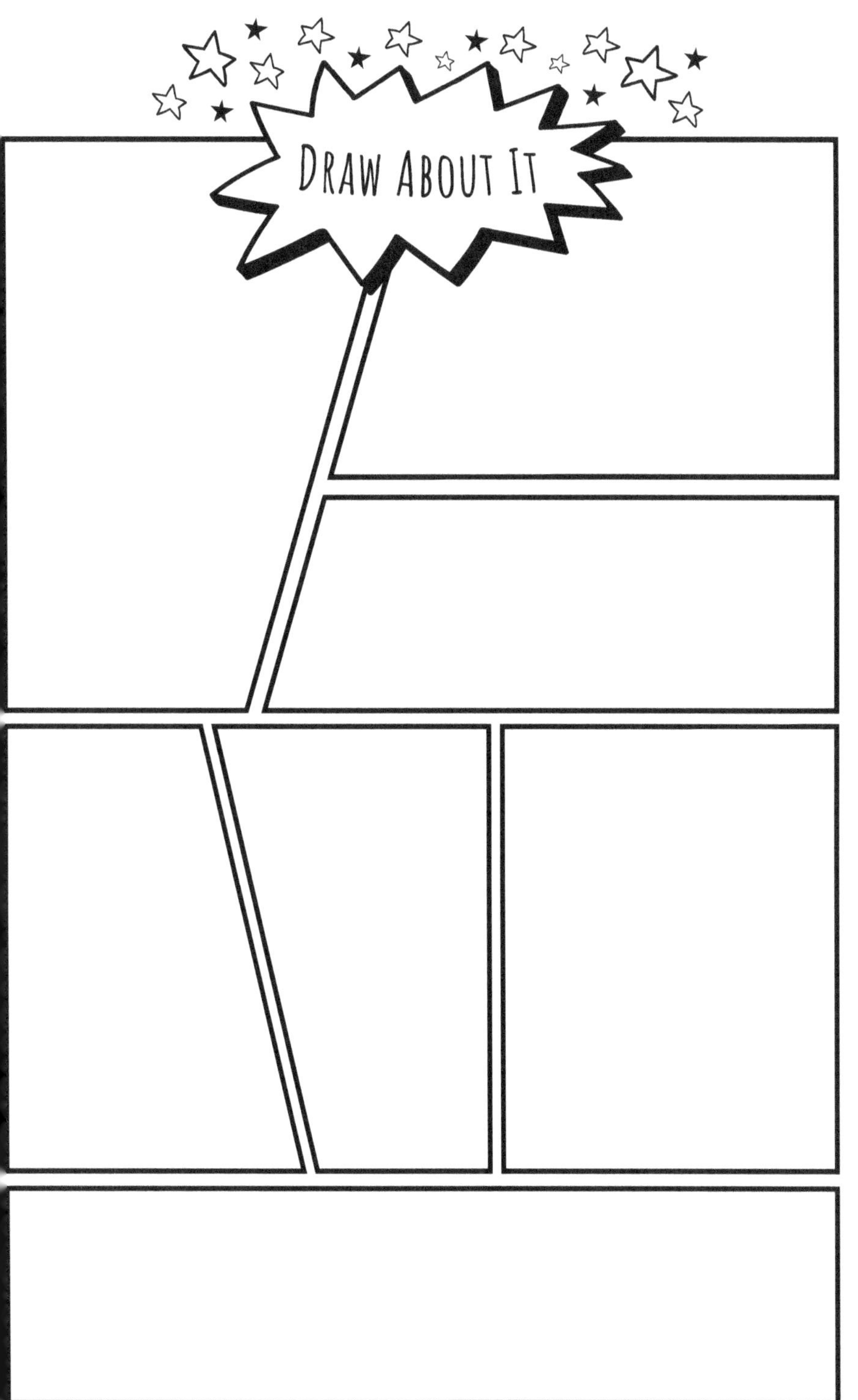

Draw About It

DATE: S M T W TH F S __ / __ / __

OVERALL TODAY WAS: ☆ ☆ ☆ ☆ ☆

👍 TODAY'S TRIUMPHS

👎 TODAY'S CHALLENGES

💡 WHAT I LEARNED FROM TODAY:

🏆 MY TOP GOAL FOR TOMORROW:

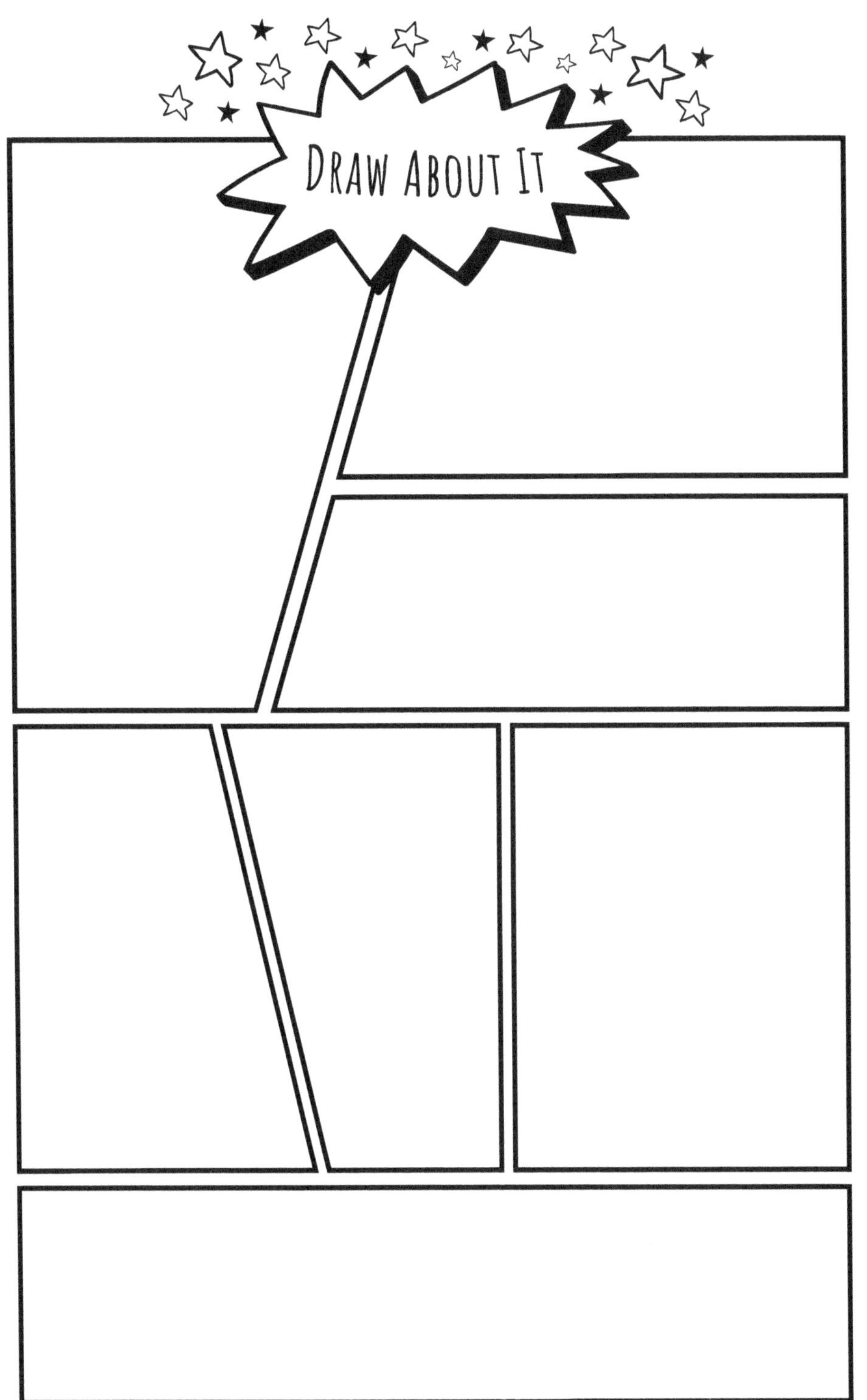
Draw About It

DATE: S M T W TH F S __/__/__

OVERALL TODAY WAS: ☆ ☆ ☆ ☆ ☆

👍 TODAY'S TRIUMPHS

👎 TODAY'S CHALLENGES

💡 WHAT I LEARNED FROM TODAY:

🏆 MY TOP GOAL FOR TOMORROW:

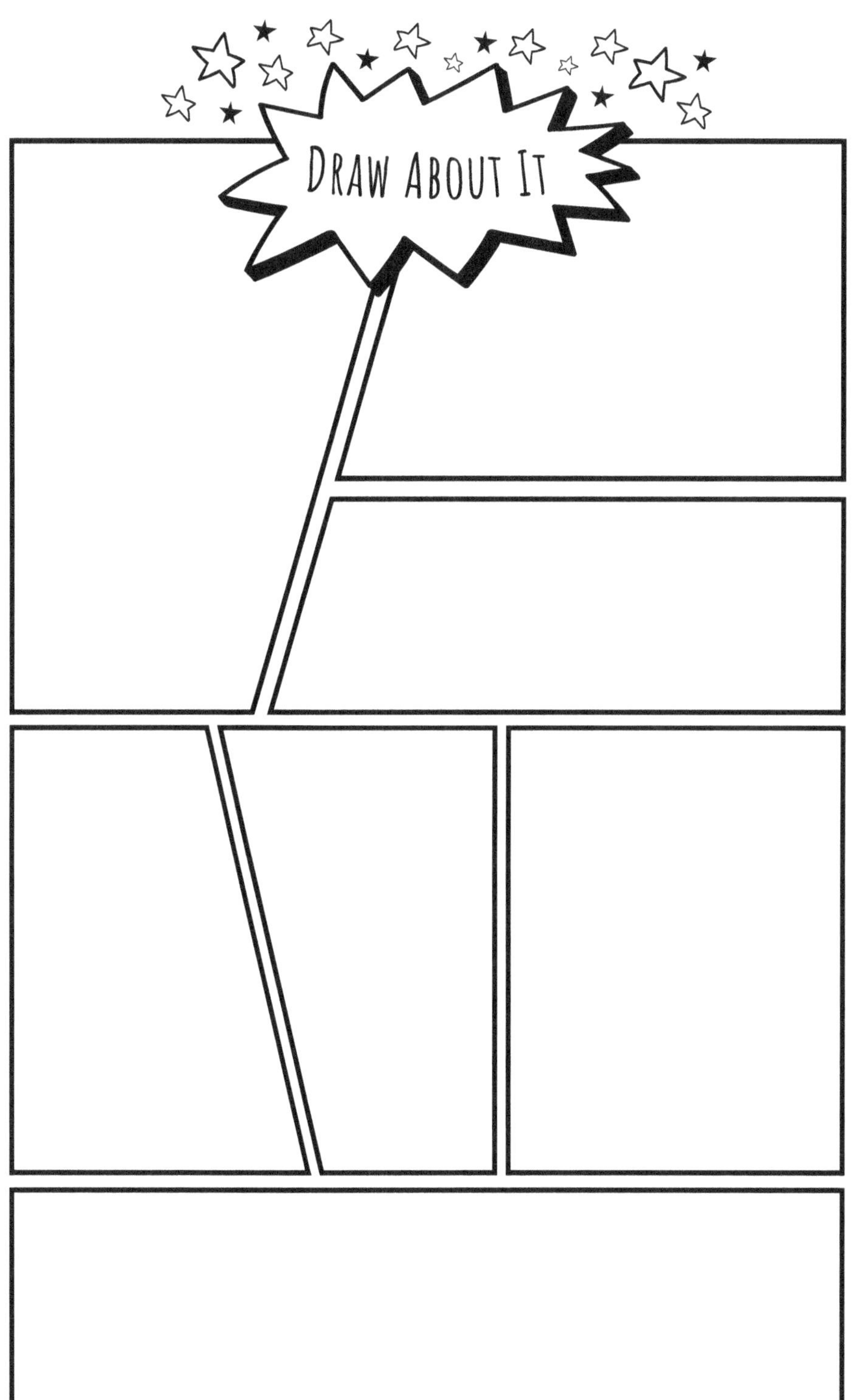
Draw About It

DATE: S M T W TH F S __/__/__

OVERALL TODAY WAS: ☆ ☆ ☆ ☆ ☆

👍 TODAY'S TRIUMPHS

👎 TODAY'S CHALLENGES

💡 WHAT I LEARNED FROM TODAY:

🏆 MY TOP GOAL FOR TOMORROW:

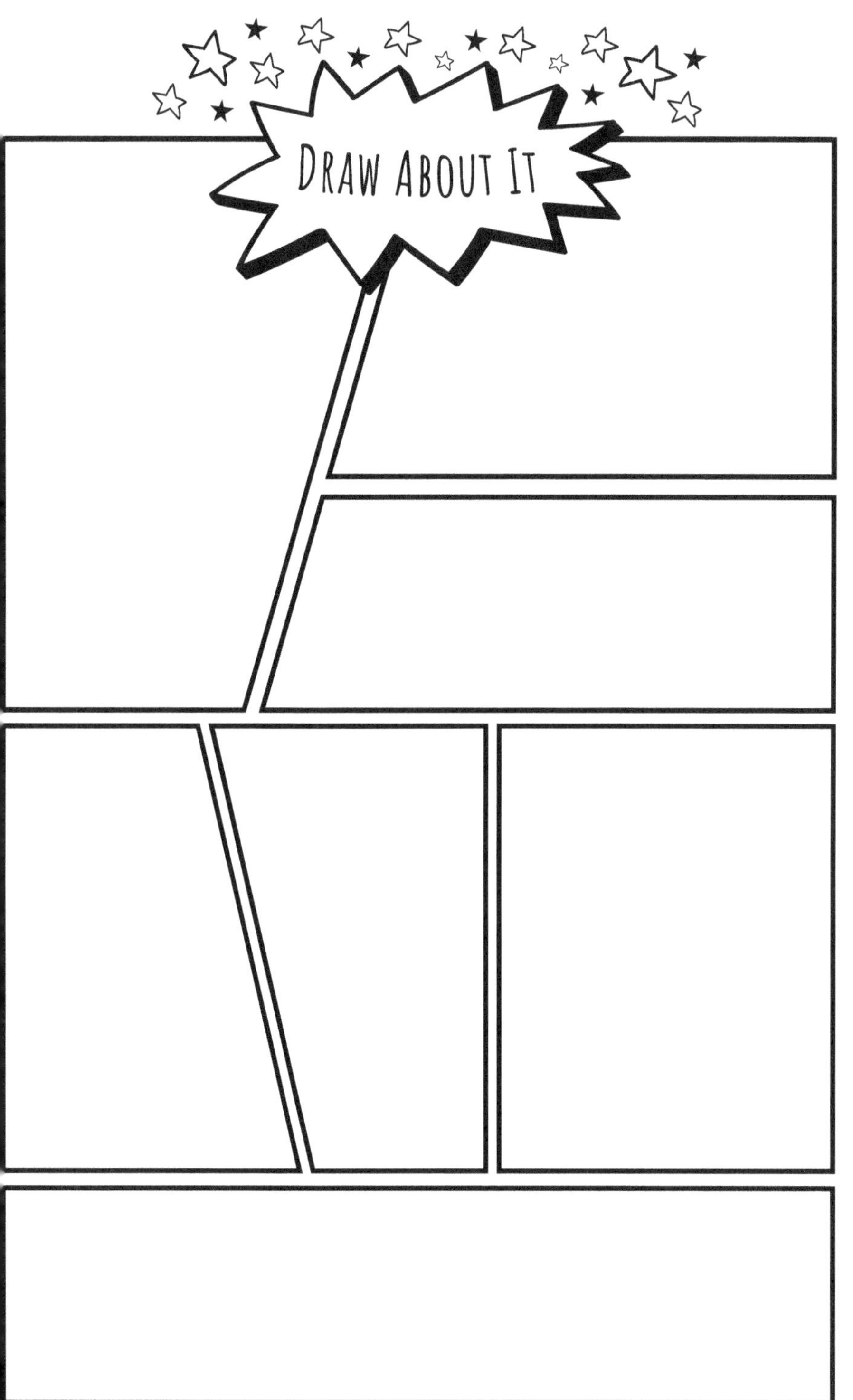

DRAW ABOUT IT

DATE: S M T W TH F S __ / __ / __

OVERALL TODAY WAS: ☆ ☆ ☆ ☆ ☆

👍 TODAY'S TRIUMPHS

👎 TODAY'S CHALLENGES

💡 WHAT I LEARNED FROM TODAY:

🏆 MY TOP GOAL FOR TOMORROW:

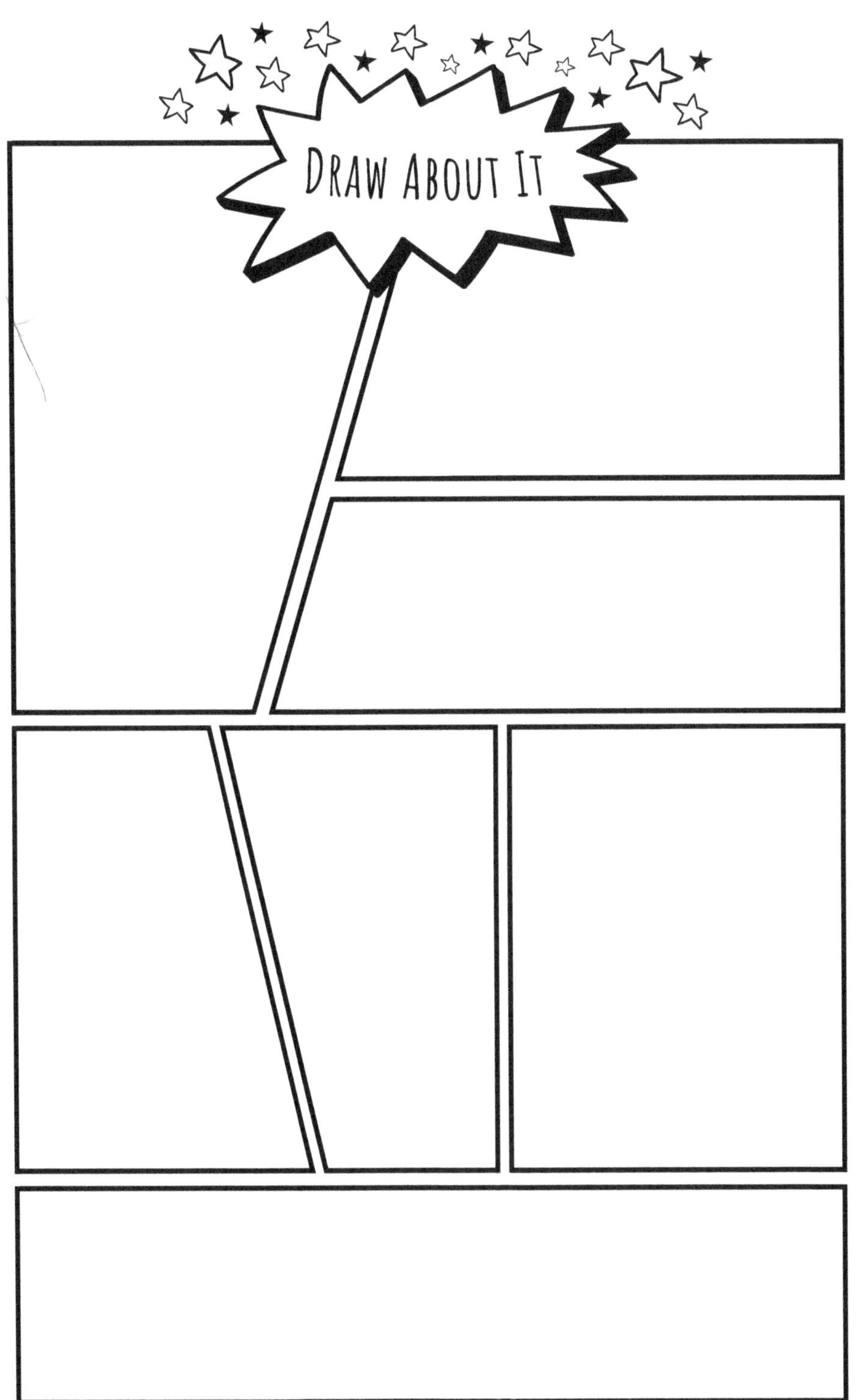
Draw About It

DATE: S M T W TH F S __ / __ / __

OVERALL TODAY WAS: ☆ ☆ ☆ ☆ ☆

👍 TODAY'S TRIUMPHS

TODAY'S CHALLENGES 👎

💡 WHAT I LEARNED FROM TODAY:

🏆 MY TOP GOAL FOR TOMORROW:

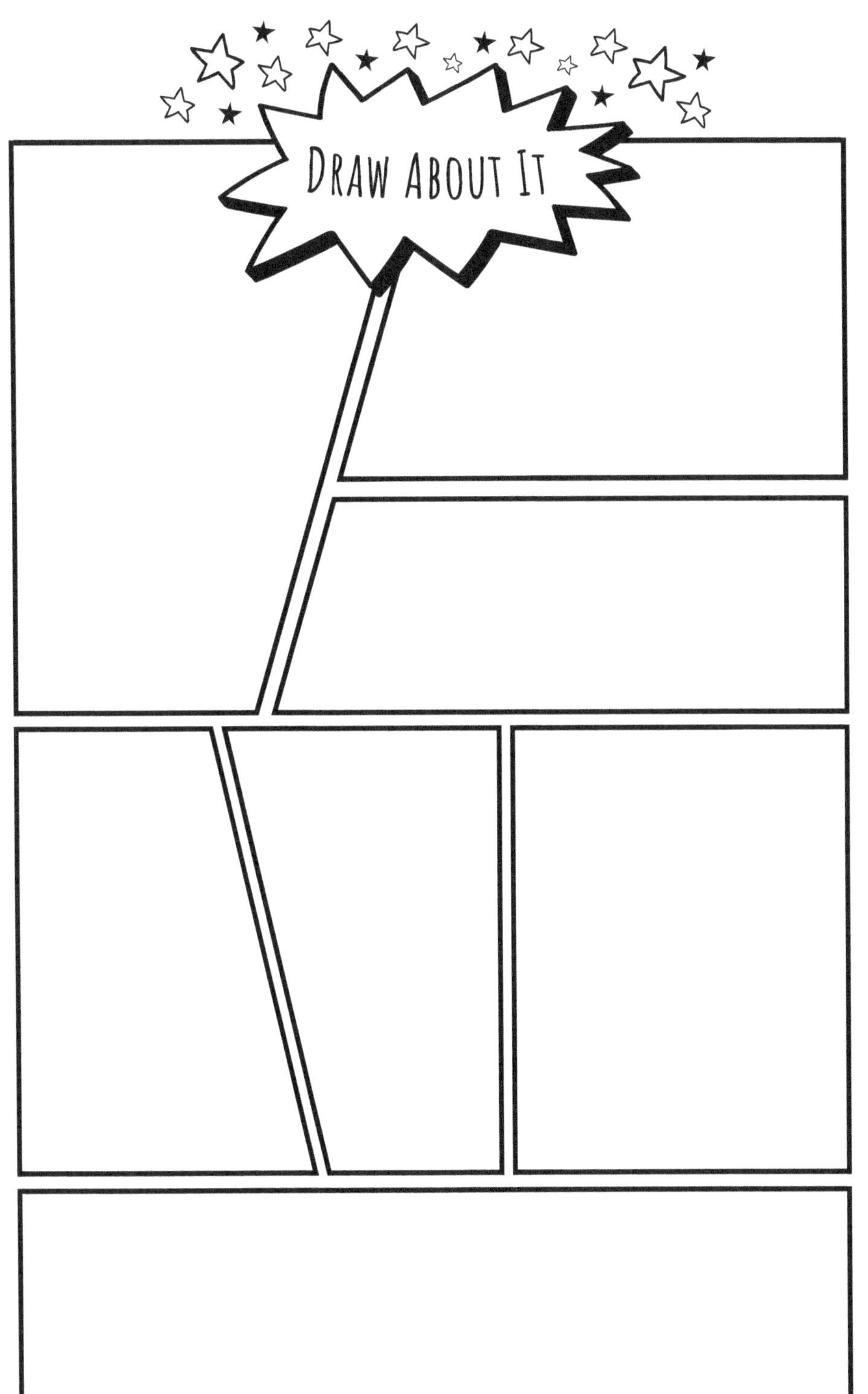

Draw About It

DATE: S M T W TH F S __ / __ / __

👍 TODAY'S TRIUMPHS

👎 TODAY'S CHALLENGES

💡 WHAT I LEARNED FROM TODAY:

🏆 MY TOP GOAL FOR TOMORROW:

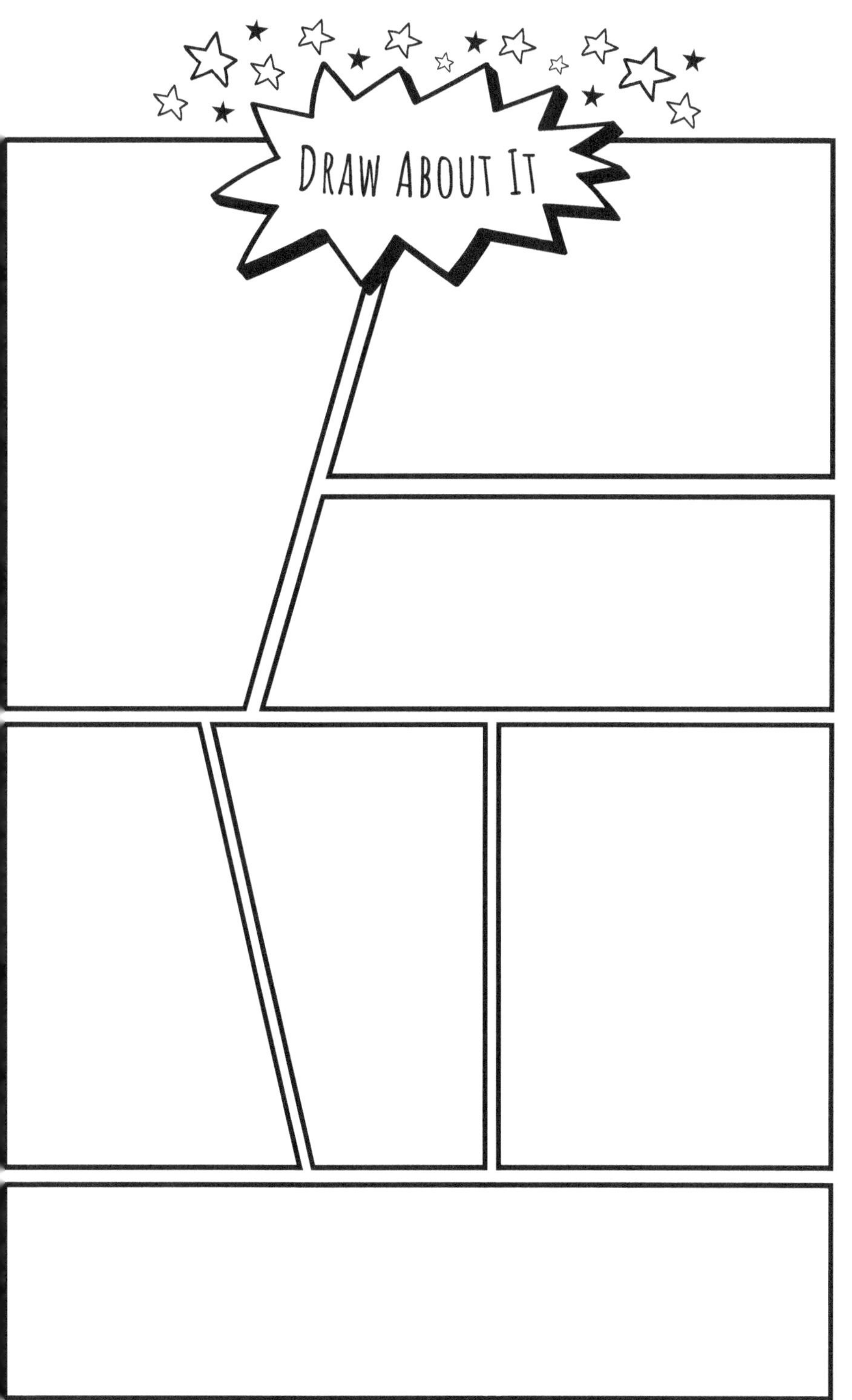
DRAW ABOUT IT

DATE: S M T W TH F S __ / __ / __

OVERALL TODAY WAS: ☆ ☆ ☆ ☆ ☆

👍 TODAY'S TRIUMPHS

👎 TODAY'S CHALLENGES

💡 WHAT I LEARNED FROM TODAY:

🏆 MY TOP GOAL FOR TOMORROW:

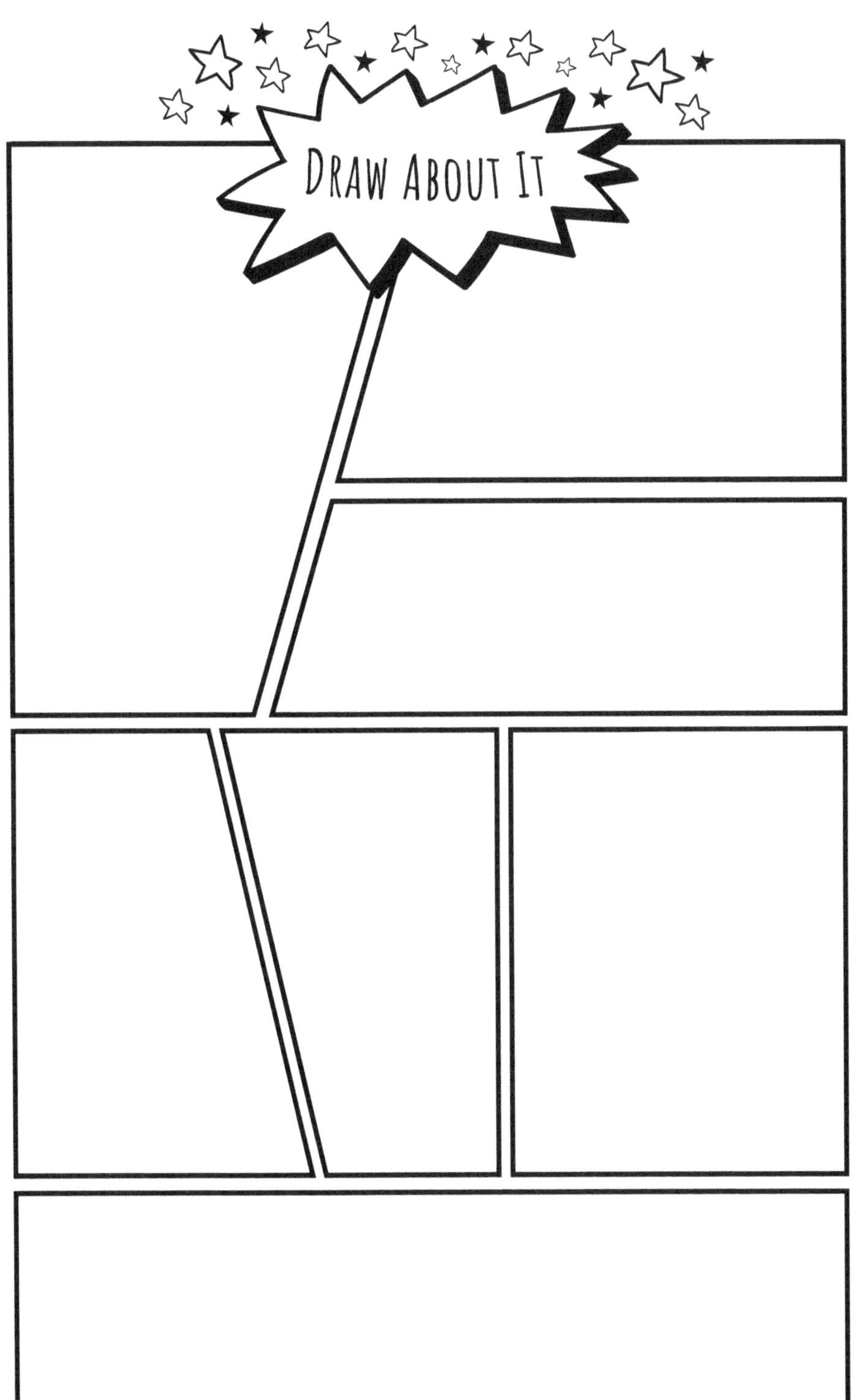
Draw About It

DATE: S M T W TH F S   __ / __ / __

OVERALL TODAY WAS: ☆ ☆ ☆ ☆ ☆

👍 TODAY'S TRIUMPHS

👎 TODAY'S CHALLENGES

💡 WHAT I LEARNED FROM TODAY:

🏆 MY TOP GOAL FOR TOMORROW:

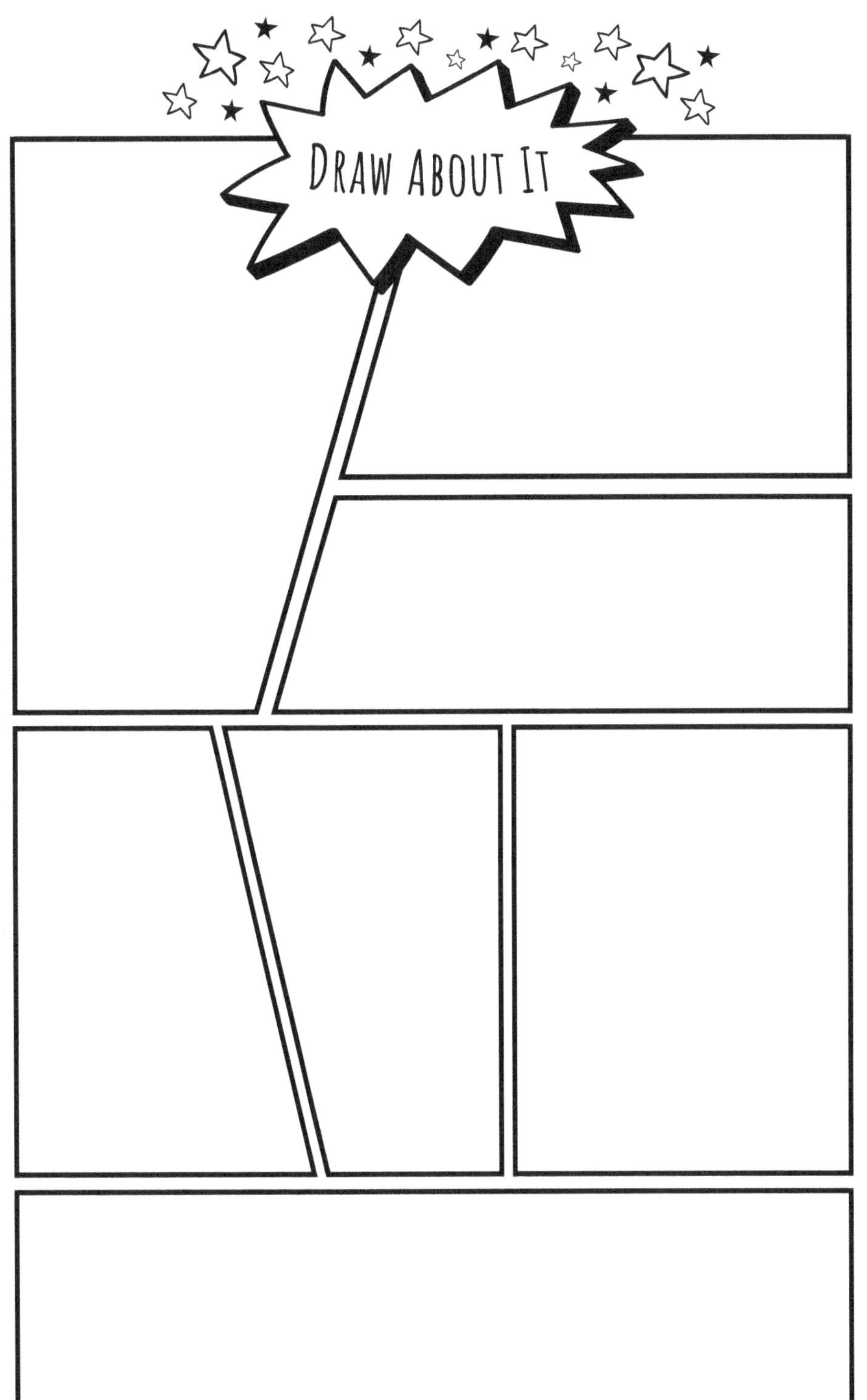
Draw About It

DATE: S M T W TH F S   __/__/__

OVERALL TODAY WAS: ☆ ☆ ☆ ☆ ☆

👍 **TODAY'S TRIUMPHS**

____

____

____

____

____

____

____

____

👎 **TODAY'S CHALLENGES**

____

____

____

____

____

____

____

💡 **WHAT I LEARNED FROM TODAY:**

____

____

🏆 **MY TOP GOAL FOR TOMORROW:**

____

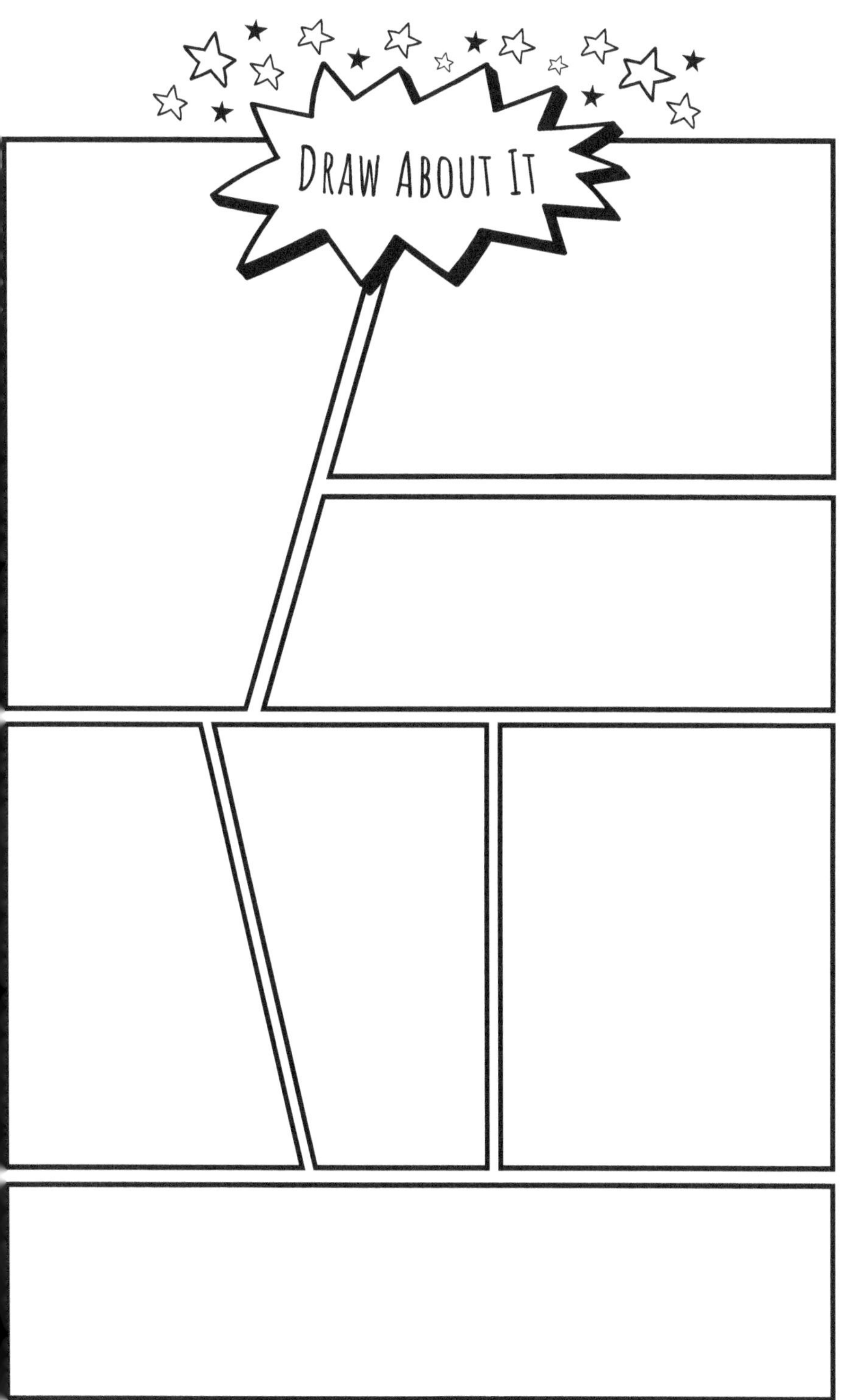
Draw About It

DATE: S M T W TH F S   __ / __ / __

OVERALL TODAY WAS: ☆ ☆ ☆ ☆ ☆

👍 TODAY'S TRIUMPHS

____
____
____
____
____
____
____
____

👎 TODAY'S CHALLENGES

____
____
____
____
____
____
____

💡 WHAT I LEARNED FROM TODAY:

____
____

🏆 MY TOP GOAL FOR TOMORROW:

____

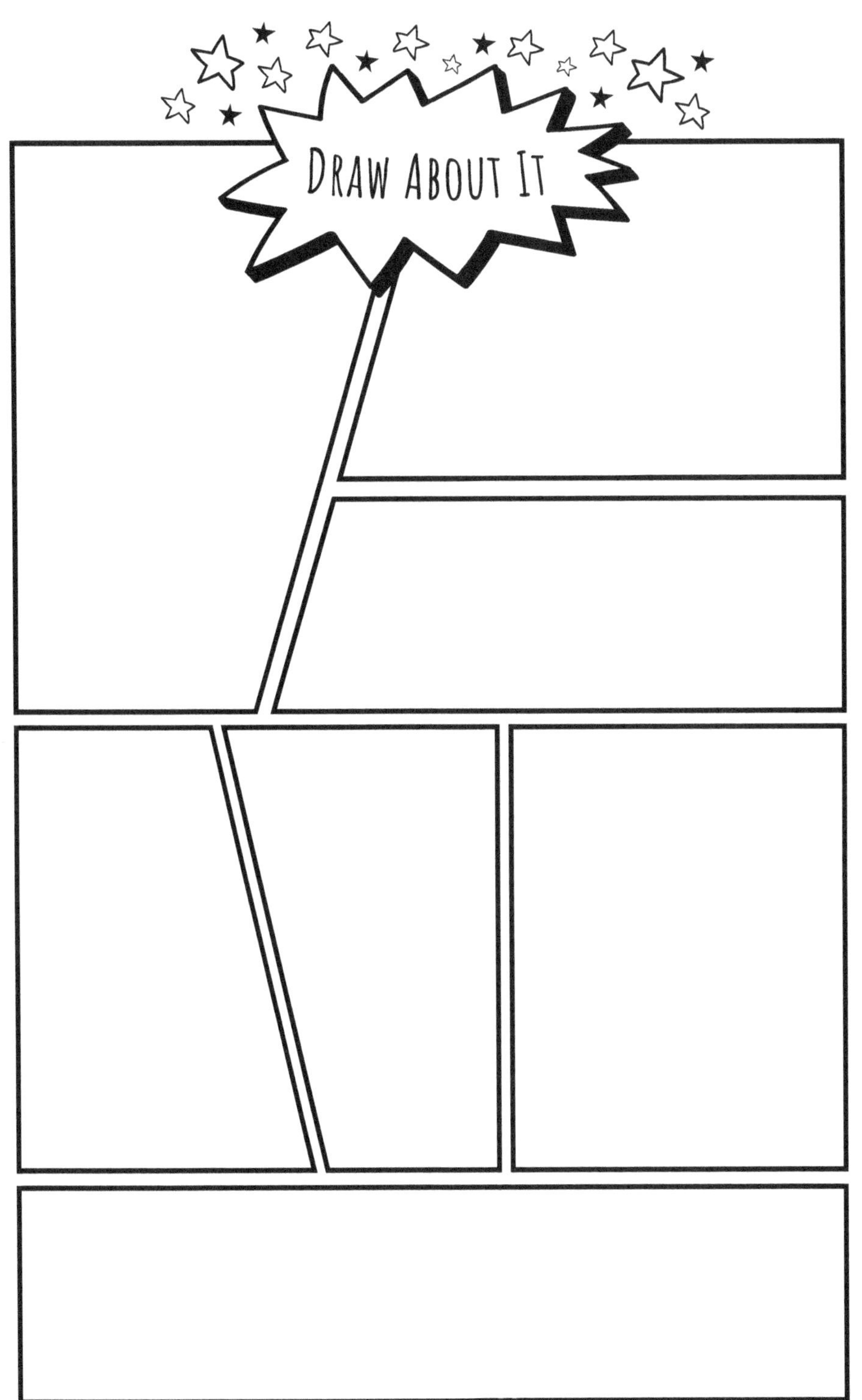
Draw About It

DATE: S M T W TH F S __ / __ / __

OVERALL TODAY WAS: ☆ ☆ ☆ ☆ ☆

👍 TODAY'S TRIUMPHS

👎 TODAY'S CHALLENGES

💡 WHAT I LEARNED FROM TODAY:

🏆 MY TOP GOAL FOR TOMORROW:

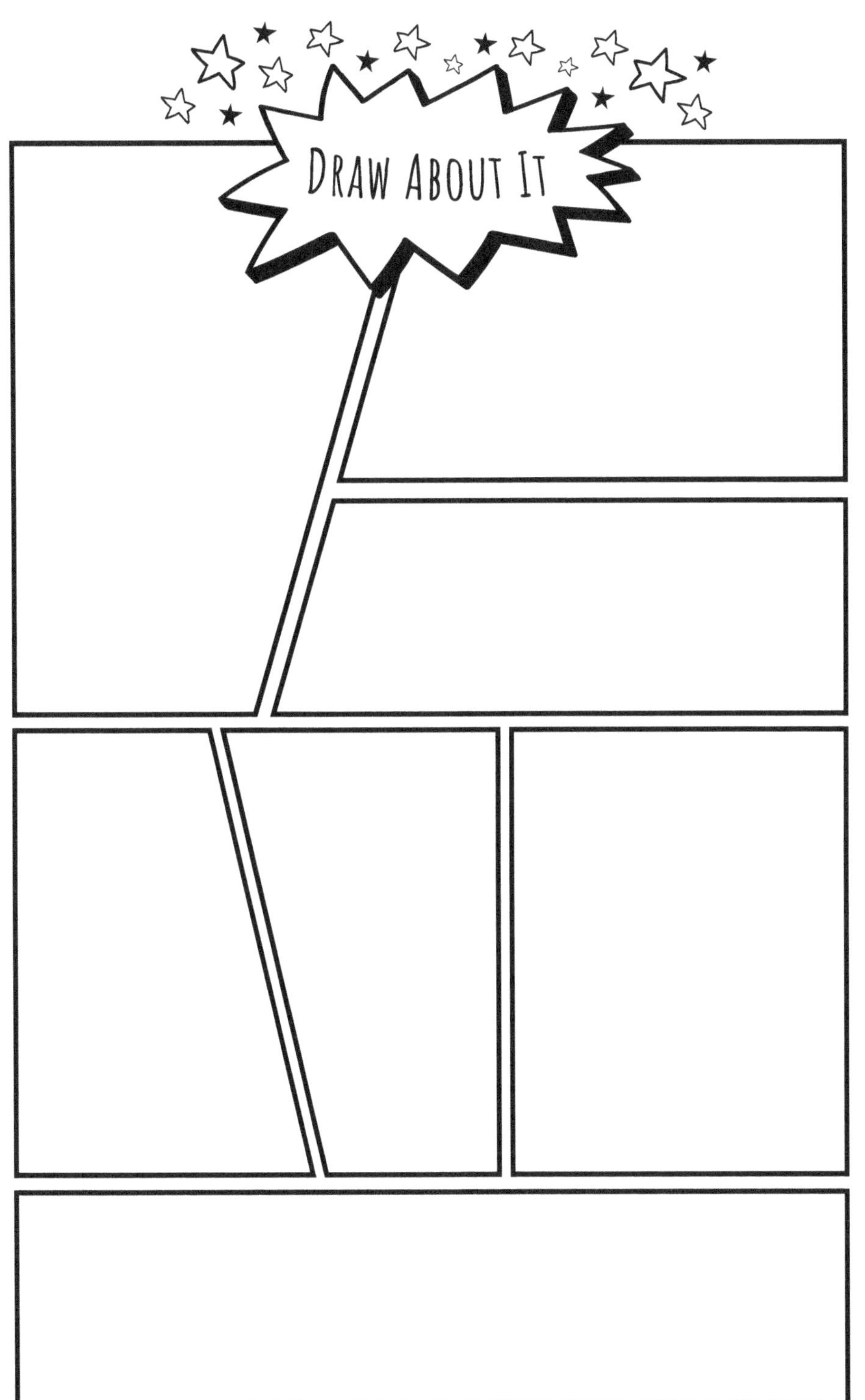
Draw About It

OVERALL TODAY WAS: ☆ ☆ ☆ ☆ ☆

👍 TODAY'S TRIUMPHS

👎 TODAY'S CHALLENGES

💡 WHAT I LEARNED FROM TODAY:

🏆 MY TOP GOAL FOR TOMORROW:

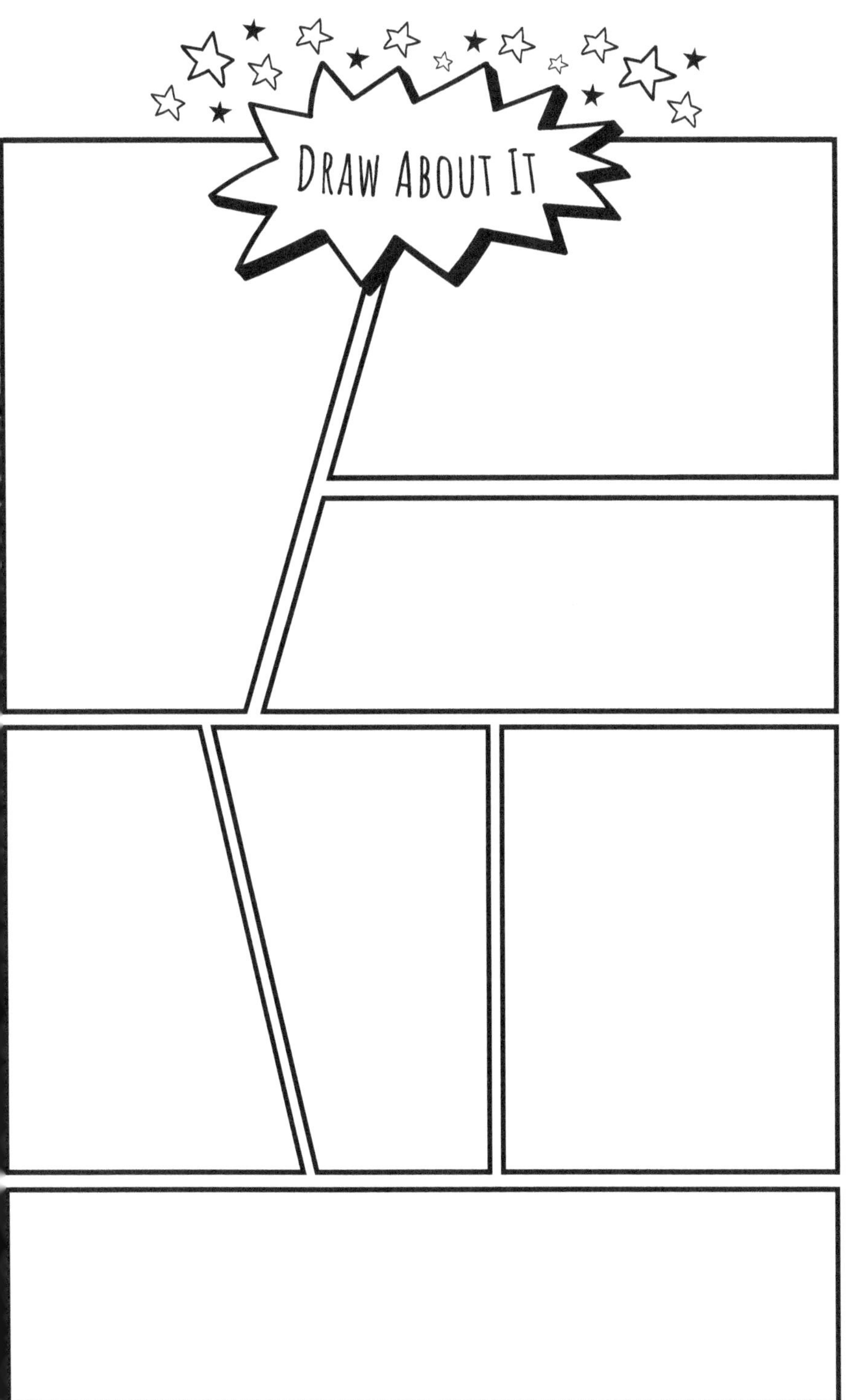

Draw About It

DATE: S M T W TH F S __ / __ / __

OVERALL TODAY WAS: ☆ ☆ ☆ ☆ ☆

👍 TODAY'S TRIUMPHS

👎 TODAY'S CHALLENGES

💡 WHAT I LEARNED FROM TODAY:

🏆 MY TOP GOAL FOR TOMORROW:

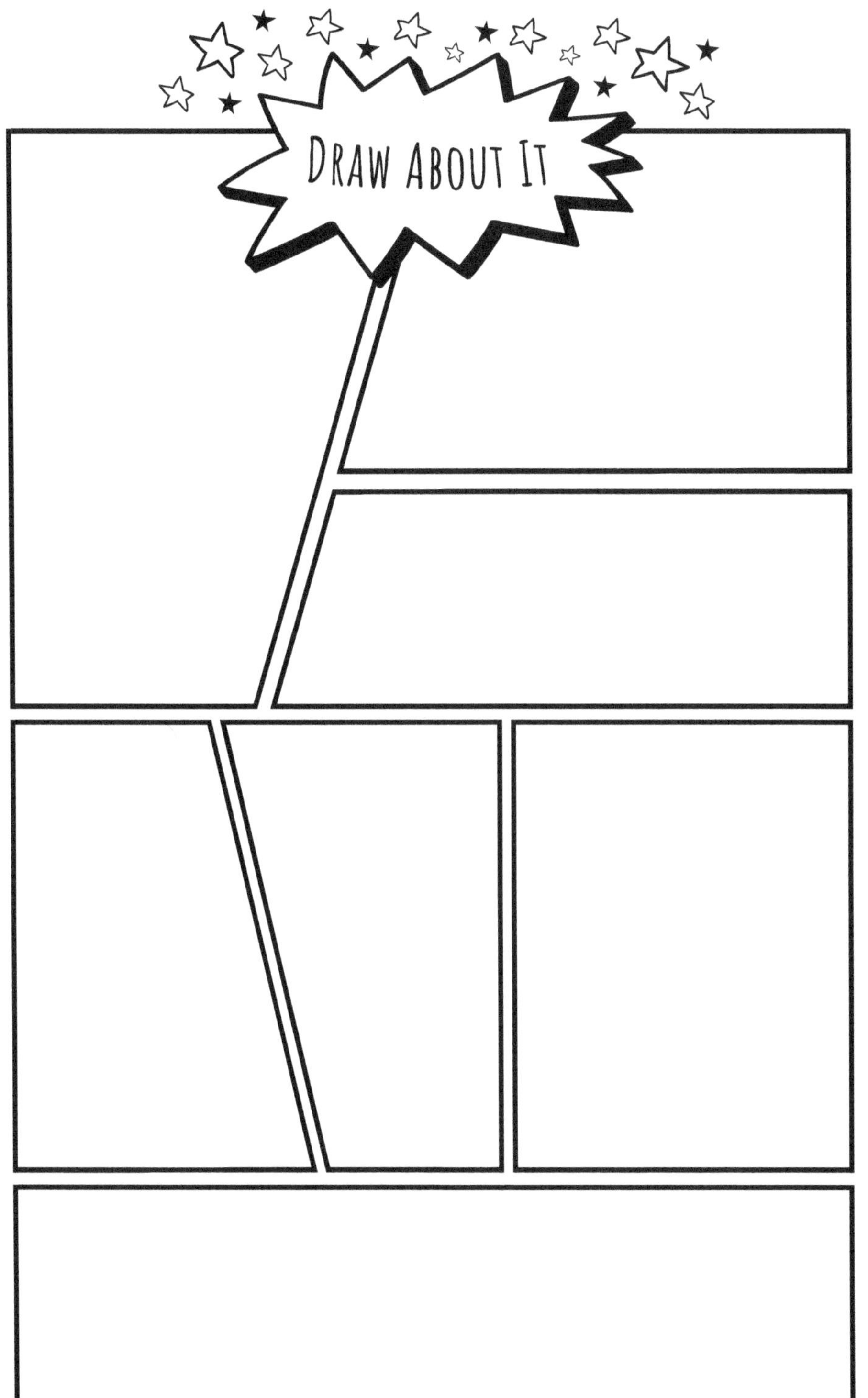
DRAW ABOUT IT

DATE: S M T W TH F S __ / __ / __

OVERALL TODAY WAS: ☆ ☆ ☆ ☆ ☆

TODAY'S TRIUMPHS

____
____
____
____
____
____
____
____

TODAY'S CHALLENGES

____
____
____
____
____
____
____

WHAT I LEARNED FROM TODAY:

____
____

MY TOP GOAL FOR TOMORROW:

____

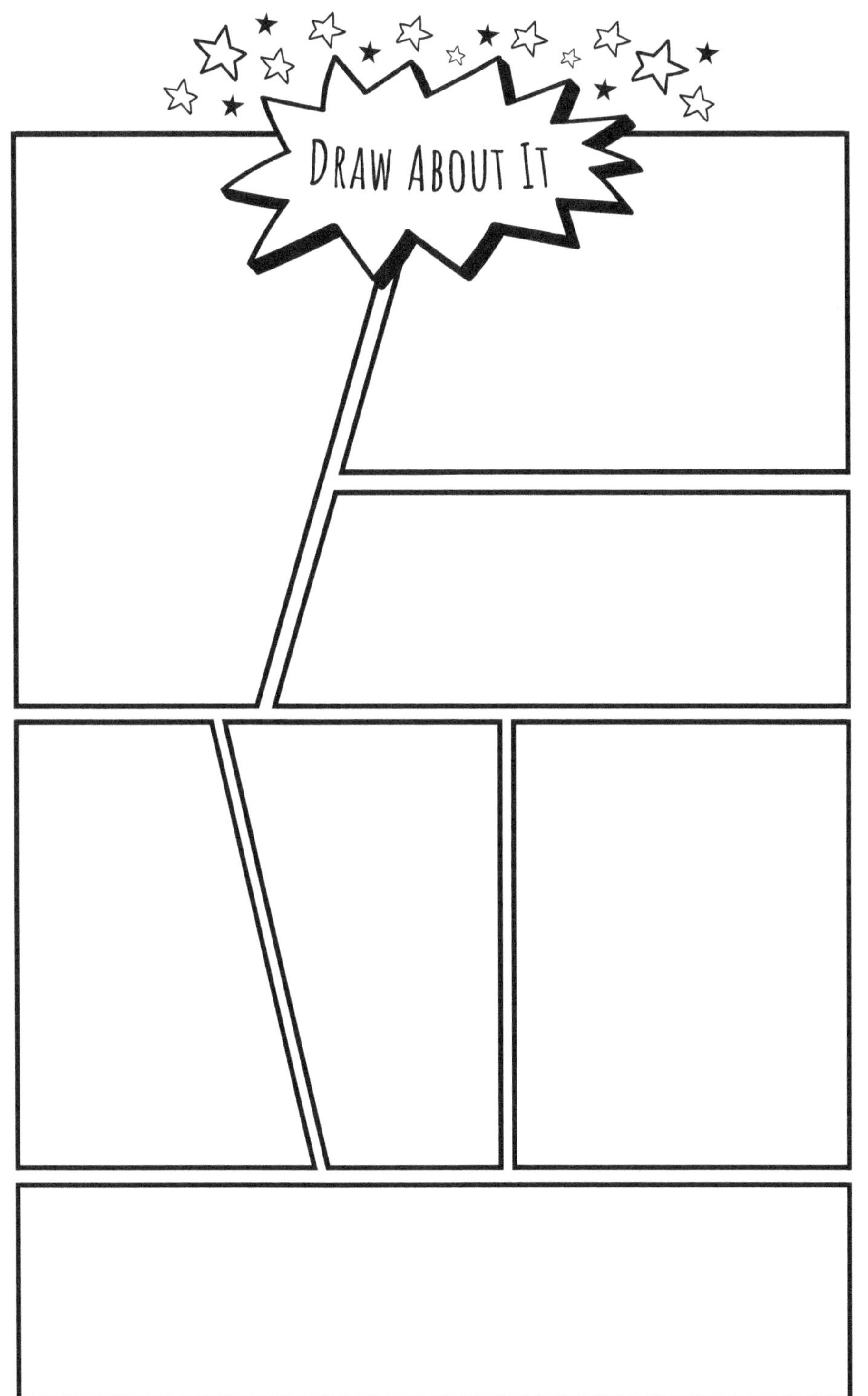
Draw About It

DATE: S M T W TH F S   __ / __ / __

OVERALL TODAY WAS: ☆ ☆ ☆ ☆ ☆

👍 TODAY'S TRIUMPHS

____

____

____

____

____

____

____

____

____

____

👎 TODAY'S CHALLENGES

____

____

____

____

____

____

____

____

____

💡 WHAT I LEARNED FROM TODAY:

____

🏆 MY TOP GOAL FOR TOMORROW:

____

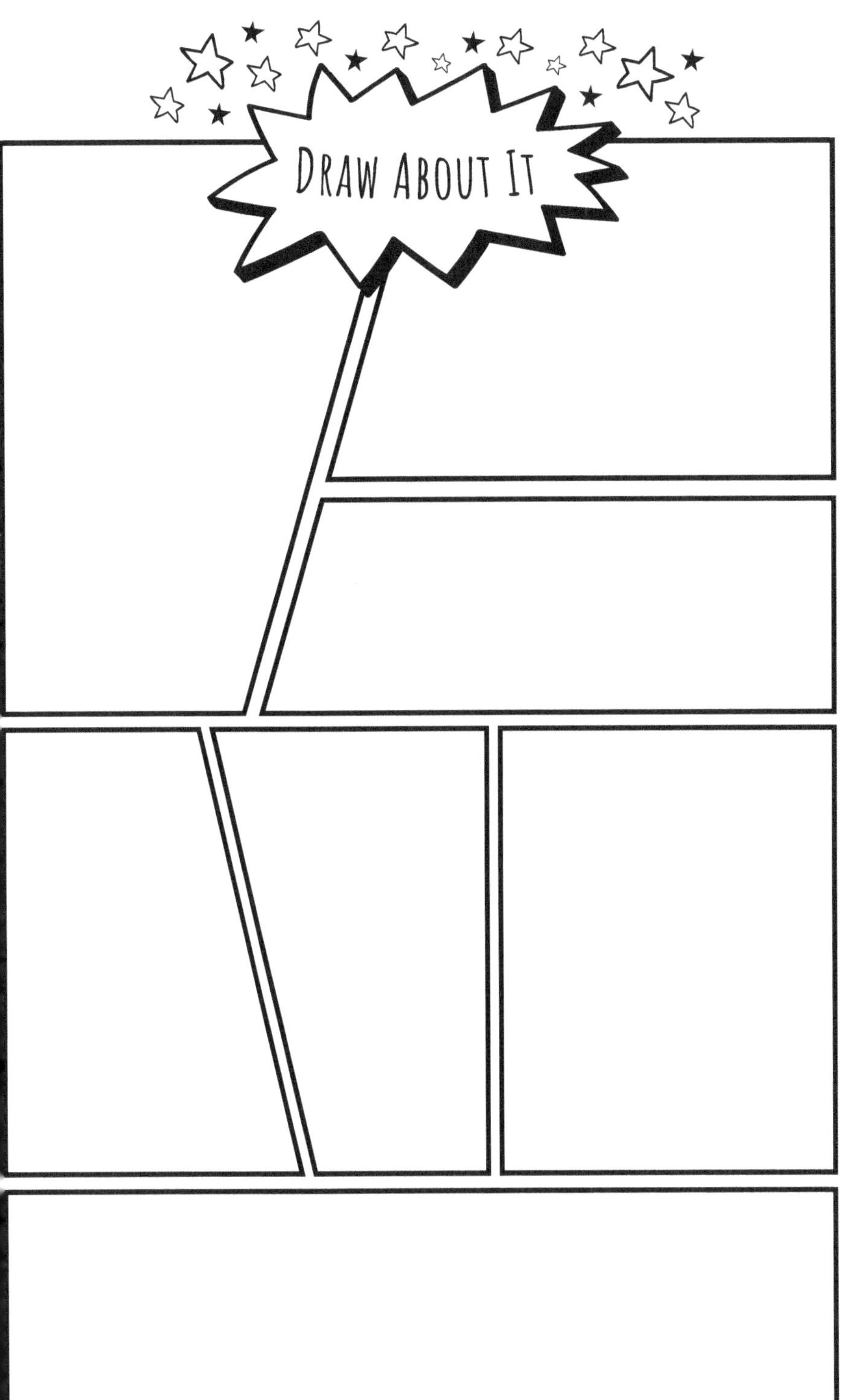
Draw About It

DATE: S M T W TH F S __ / __ / __

OVERALL TODAY WAS: ☆ ☆ ☆ ☆ ☆

👍 TODAY'S TRIUMPHS

👎 TODAY'S CHALLENGES

💡 WHAT I LEARNED FROM TODAY:

🏆 MY TOP GOAL FOR TOMORROW:

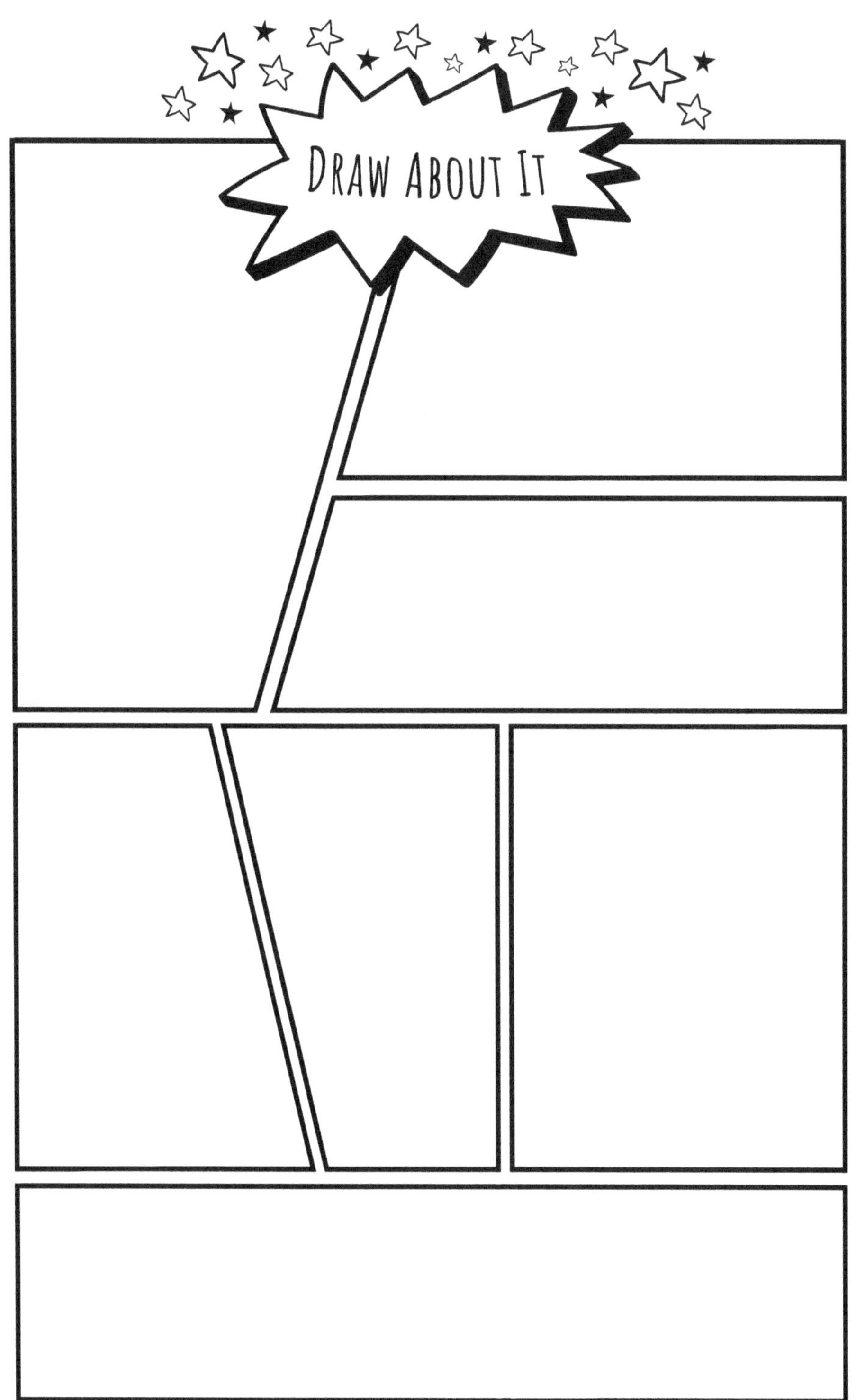Draw About It

DATE: S M T W TH F S __ / __ / __

OVERALL TODAY WAS: ☆ ☆ ☆ ☆ ☆

👍 TODAY'S TRIUMPHS

____
____
____
____
____
____
____
____
____
____

👎 TODAY'S CHALLENGES

____
____
____
____
____
____
____
____

💡 WHAT I LEARNED FROM TODAY:

____
____

🏆 MY TOP GOAL FOR TOMORROW:

____
____

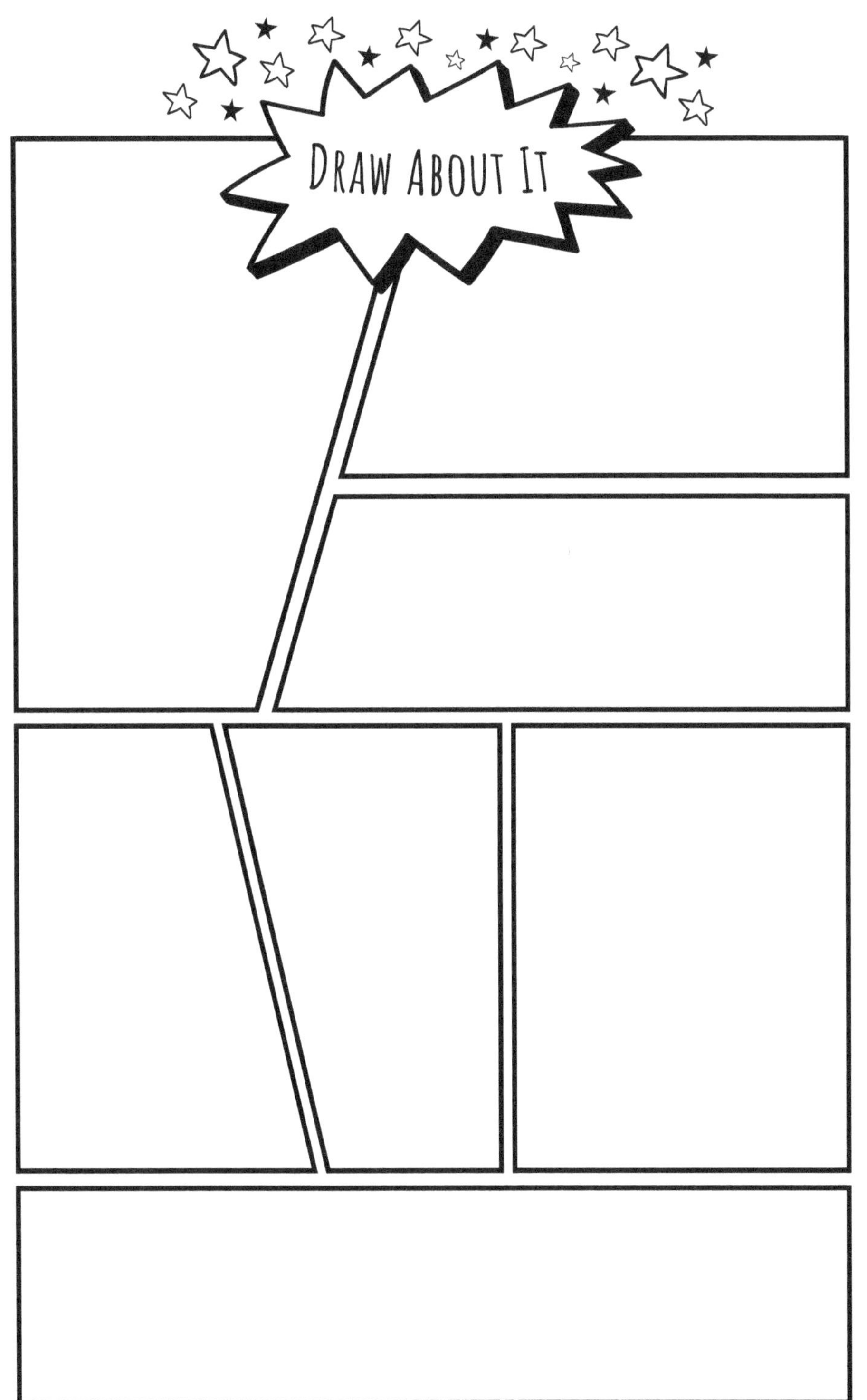
Draw About It

DATE: S M T W TH F S __ / __ / __

OVERALL TODAY WAS: ☆ ☆ ☆ ☆ ☆

👍 TODAY'S TRIUMPHS

👎 TODAY'S CHALLENGES

💡 WHAT I LEARNED FROM TODAY:

🏆 MY TOP GOAL FOR TOMORROW:

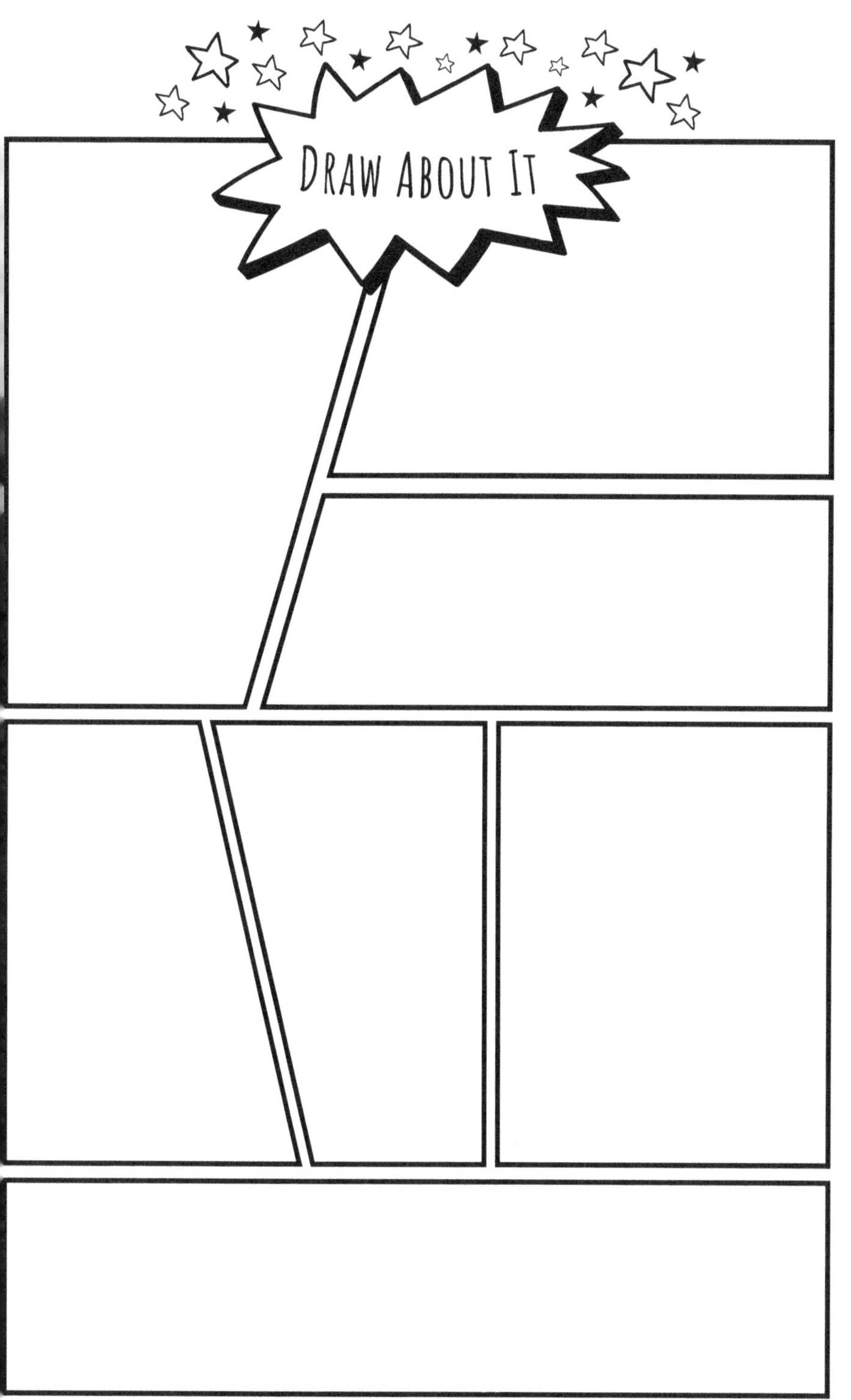

Draw About It

DATE: S M T W TH F S __ / __ / __

OVERALL TODAY WAS: ☆ ☆ ☆ ☆ ☆

👍 TODAY'S TRIUMPHS

👎 TODAY'S CHALLENGES

💡 WHAT I LEARNED FROM TODAY:

🏆 MY TOP GOAL FOR TOMORROW:

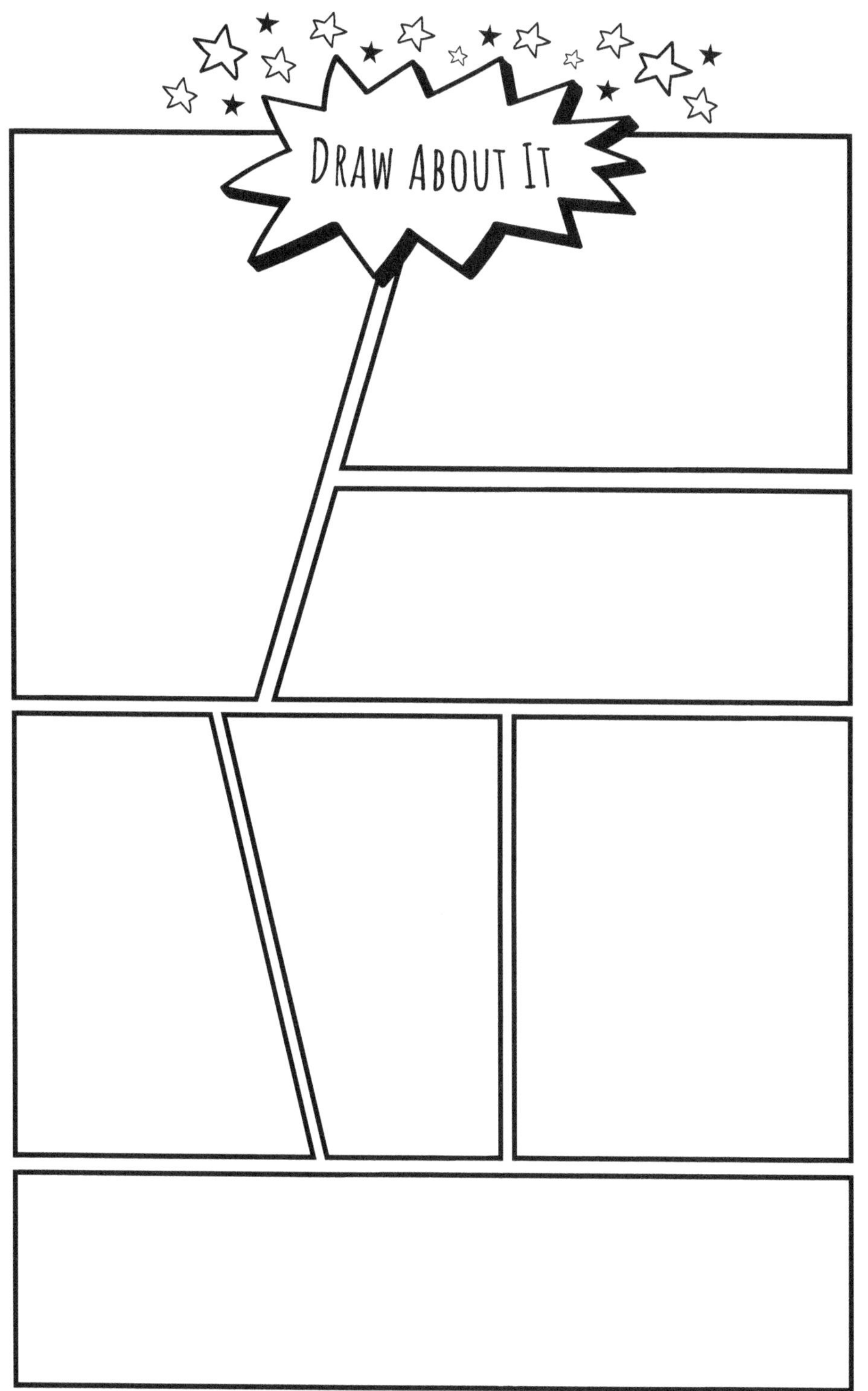
Draw About It

DATE: S M T W TH F S __ / __ / __

OVERALL TODAY WAS: ☆ ☆ ☆ ☆ ☆

👍 TODAY'S TRIUMPHS

👎 TODAY'S CHALLENGES

💡 WHAT I LEARNED FROM TODAY:

🏆 MY TOP GOAL FOR TOMORROW:

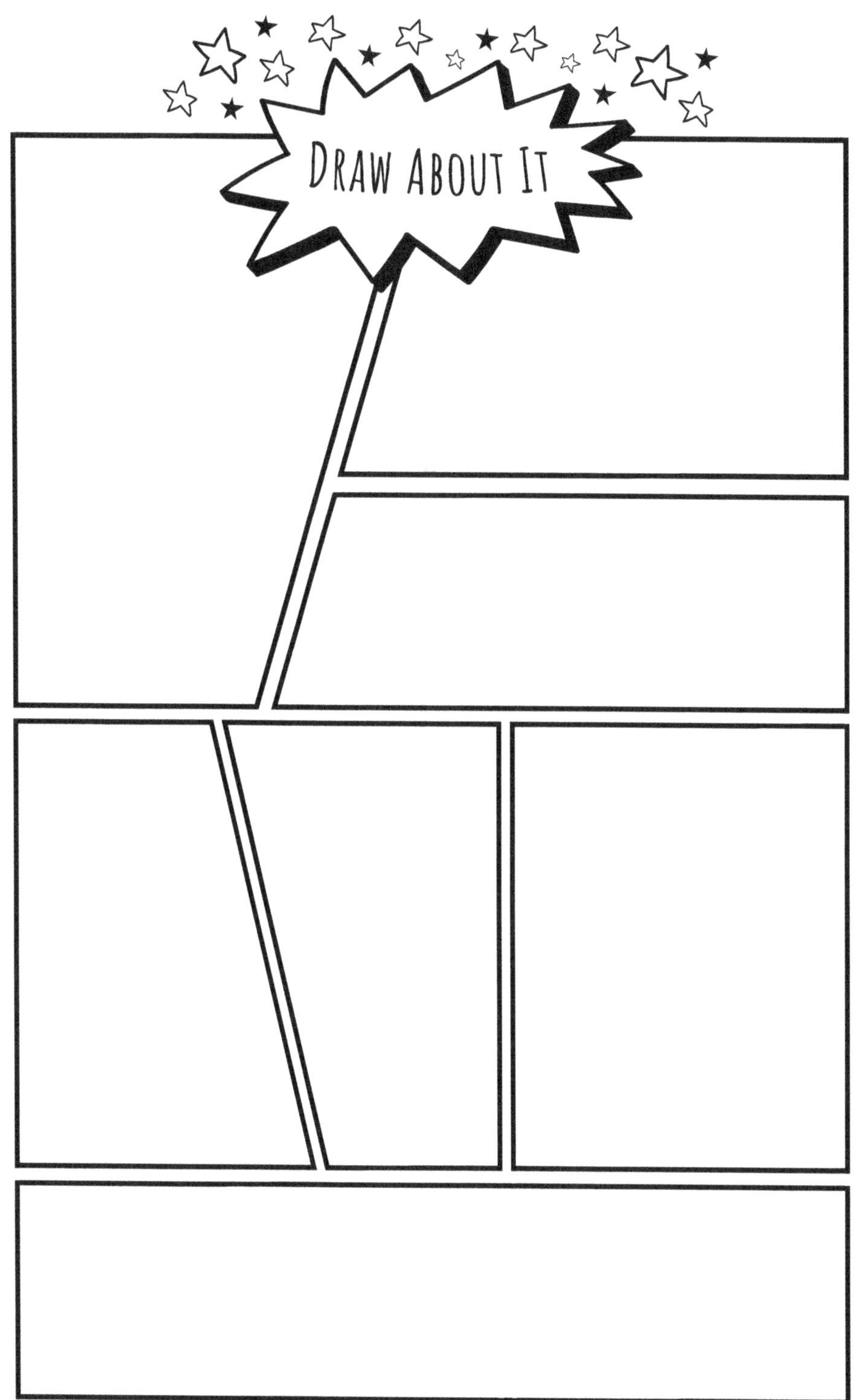

Draw About It

DATE: S M T W TH F S   __ / __ / __

OVERALL TODAY WAS: ☆ ☆ ☆ ☆ ☆

👍 TODAY'S TRIUMPHS

👎 TODAY'S CHALLENGES

💡 WHAT I LEARNED FROM TODAY:

🏆 MY TOP GOAL FOR TOMORROW:

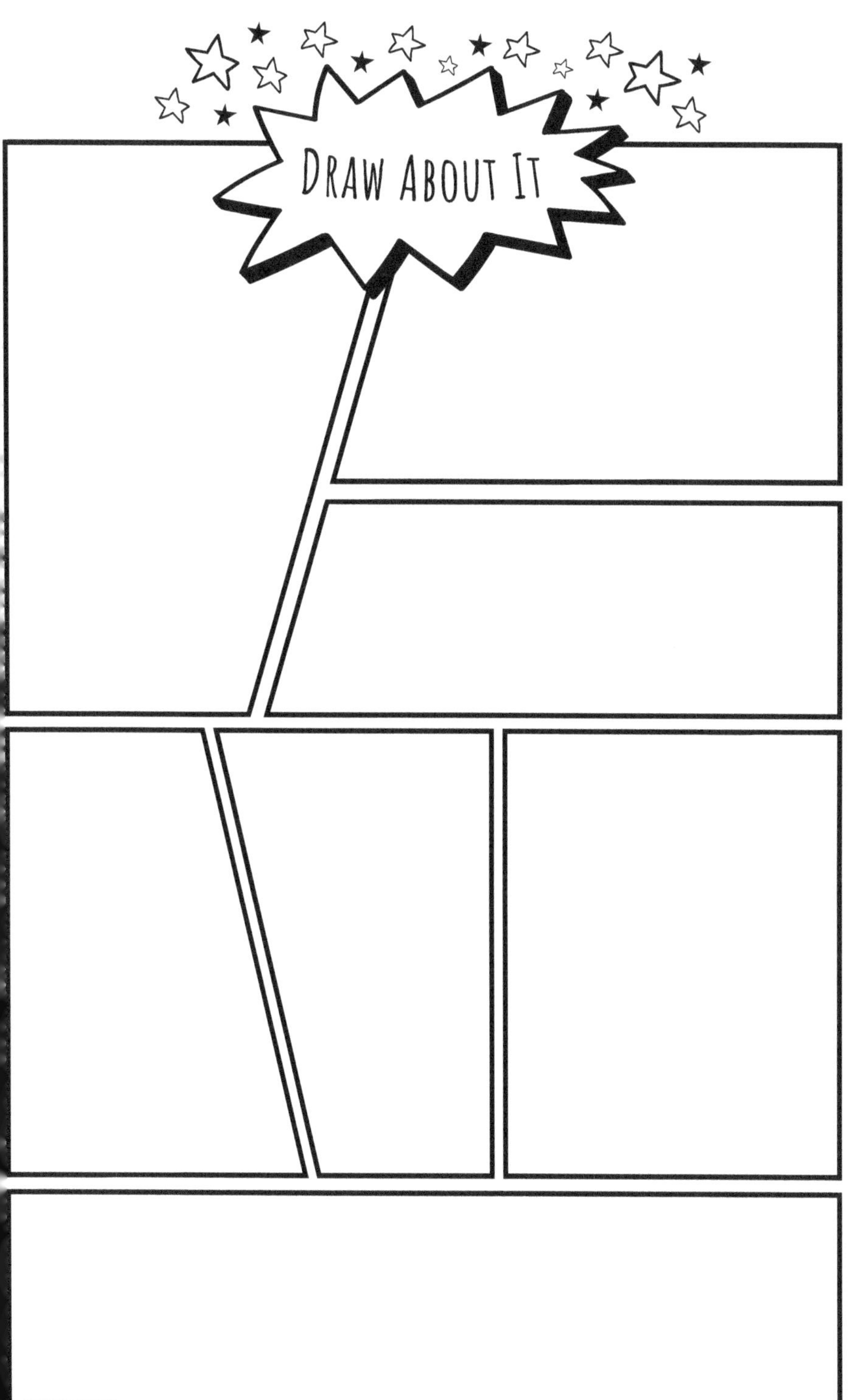
Draw About It

DATE: S M T W TH F S __ / __ / __

OVERALL TODAY WAS: ☆ ☆ ☆ ☆ ☆

👍 TODAY'S TRIUMPHS

____
____
____
____
____
____
____
____

👎 TODAY'S CHALLENGES

____
____
____
____
____
____
____
____

💡 WHAT I LEARNED FROM TODAY:

____
____

🏆 MY TOP GOAL FOR TOMORROW:

____

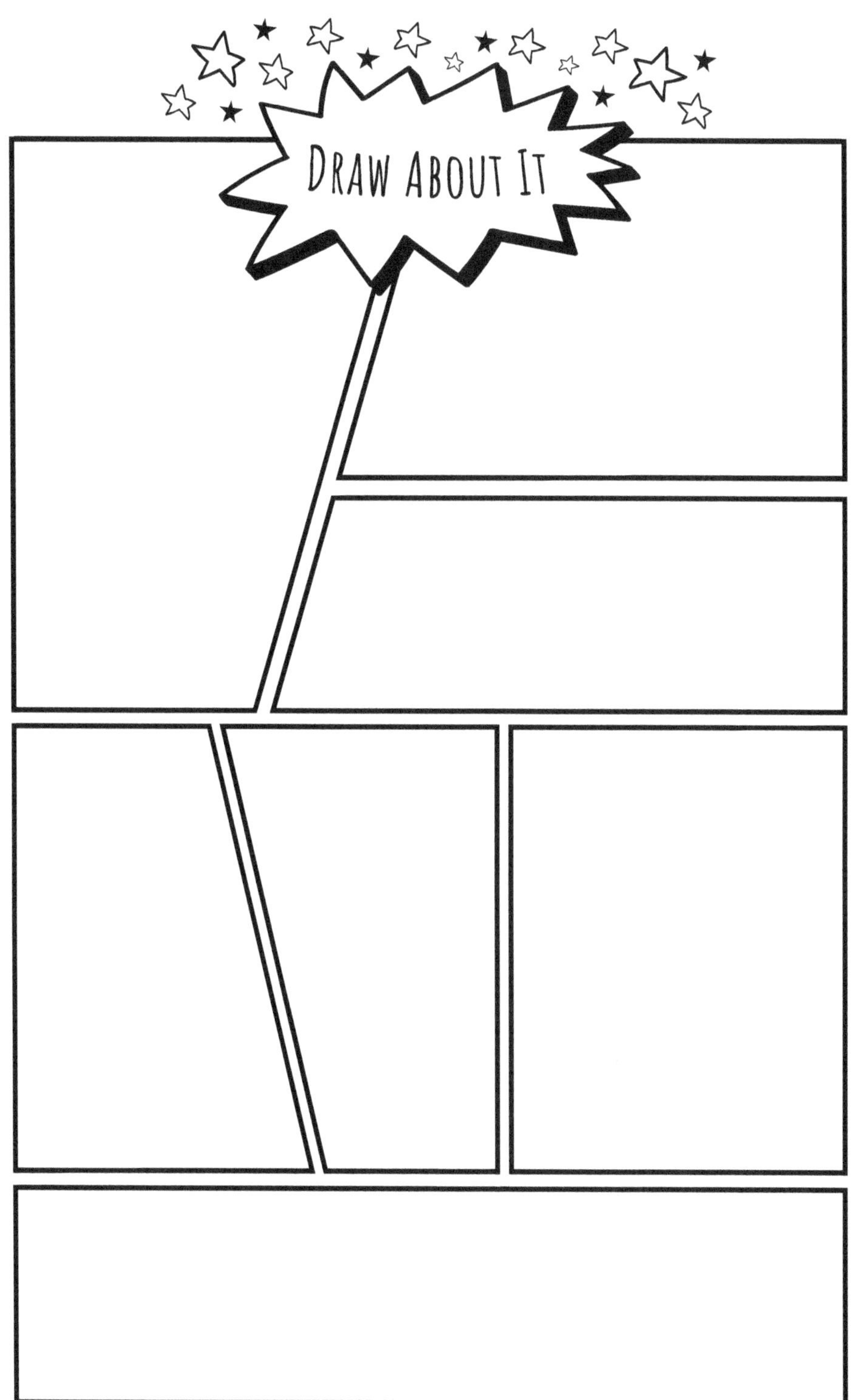
Draw About It

DATE: S M T W TH F S   __ / __ / __

OVERALL TODAY WAS: ☆ ☆ ☆ ☆ ☆

👍 TODAY'S TRIUMPHS

👎 TODAY'S CHALLENGES

💡 WHAT I LEARNED FROM TODAY:

🏆 MY TOP GOAL FOR TOMORROW:

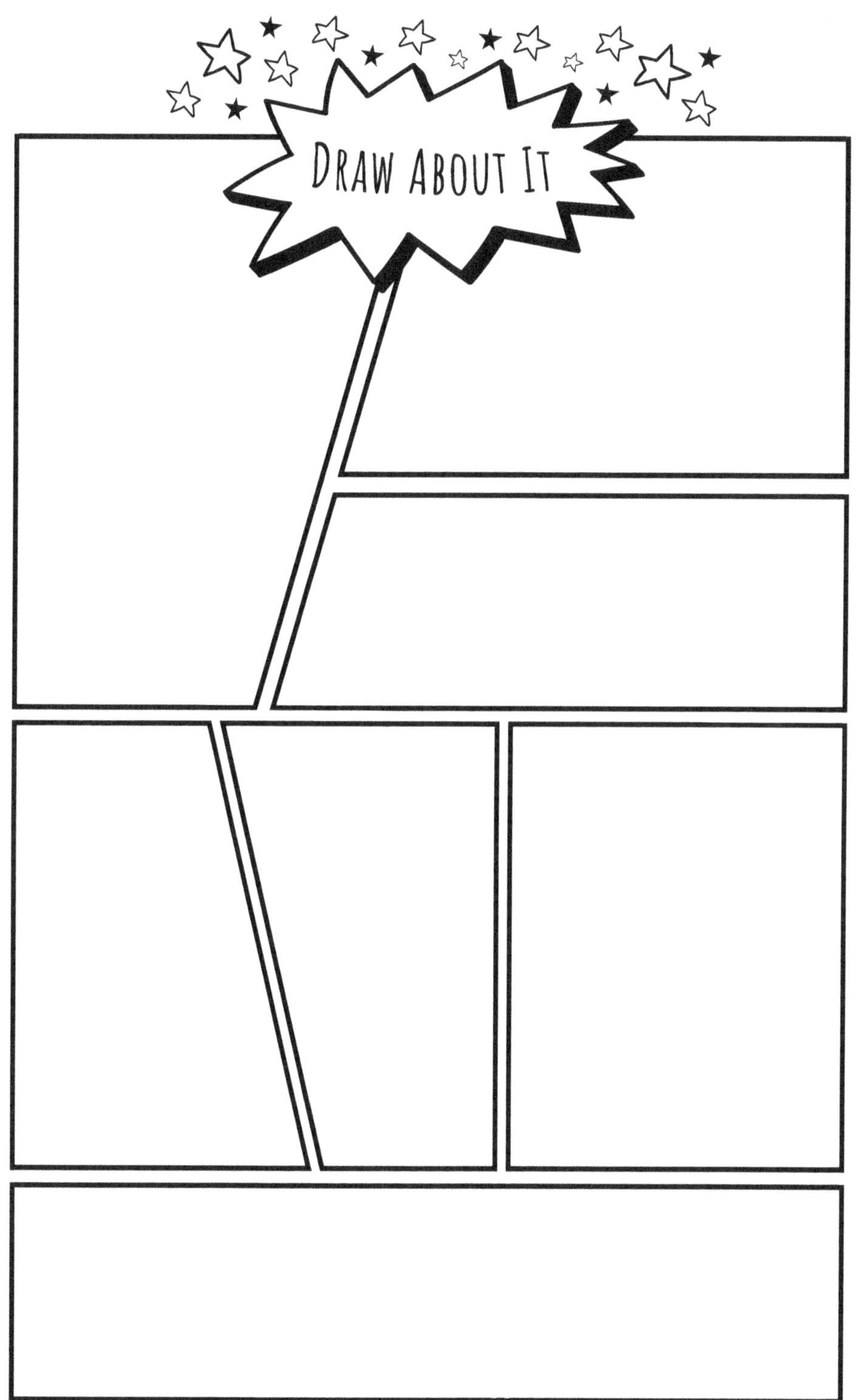
Draw About It

DATE: S M T W TH F S __ / __ / __

OVERALL TODAY WAS: ☆ ☆ ☆ ☆ ☆

👍 TODAY'S TRIUMPHS

👎 TODAY'S CHALLENGES

💡 WHAT I LEARNED FROM TODAY:

🏆 MY TOP GOAL FOR TOMORROW:

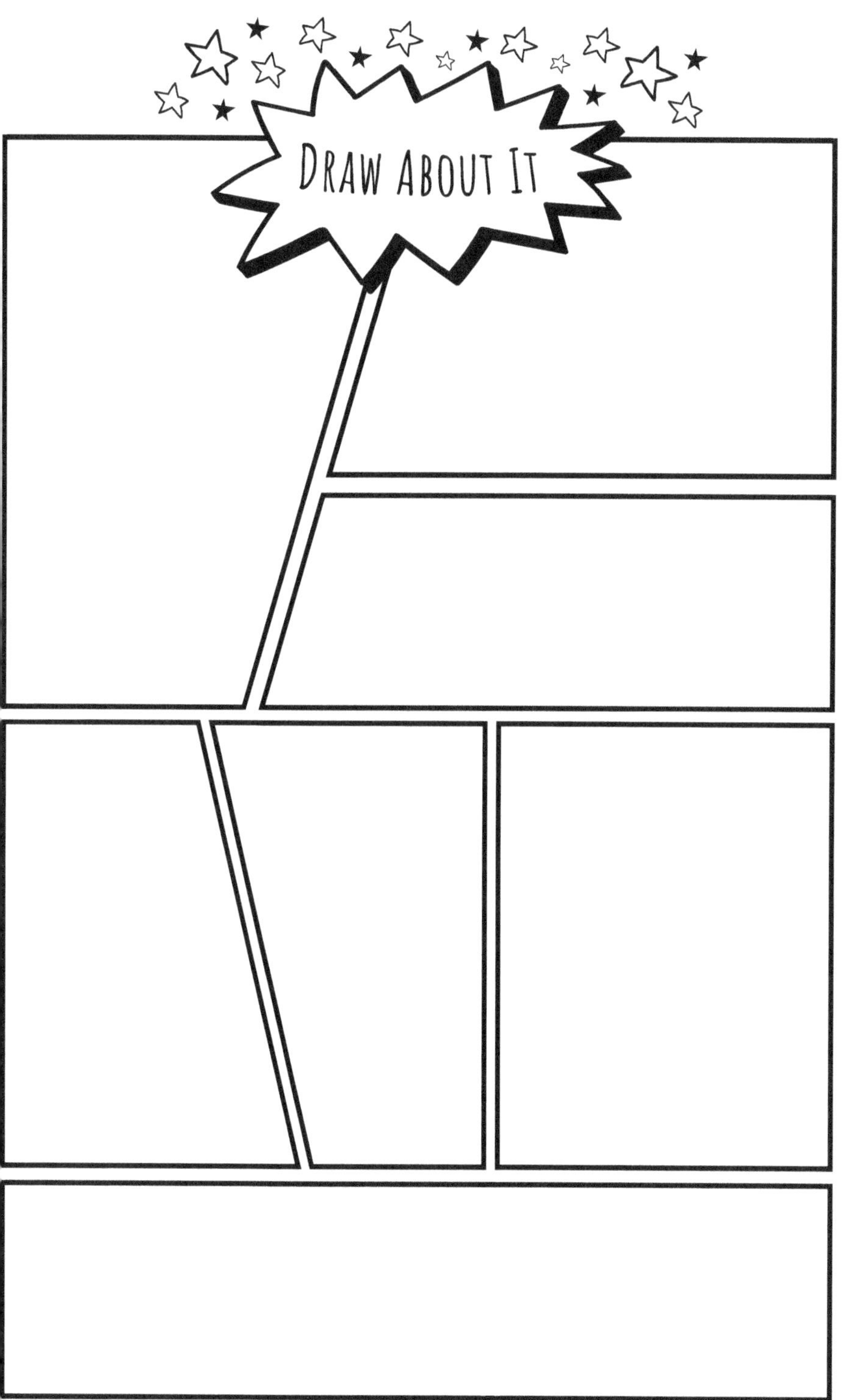

DRAW ABOUT IT

DATE: S M T W TH F S __ / __ /__

OVERALL TODAY WAS: ☆ ☆ ☆ ☆ ☆

👍 TODAY'S TRIUMPHS

👎 TODAY'S CHALLENGES

★

💡 WHAT I LEARNED FROM TODAY:

🏆 MY TOP GOAL FOR TOMORROW:

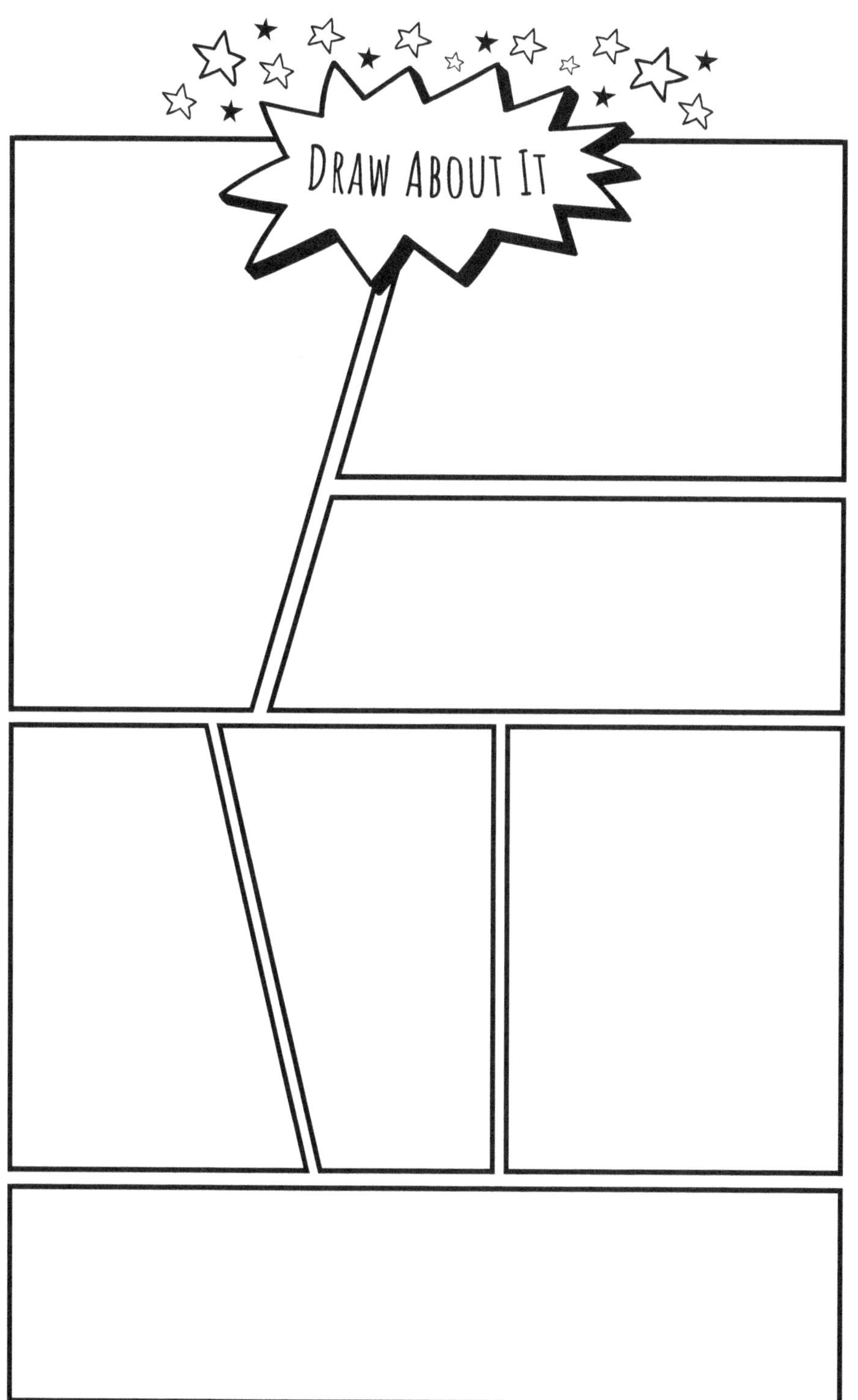
Draw About It

DATE: S M T W TH F S __ / __ / __

OVERALL TODAY WAS: ☆ ☆ ☆ ☆ ☆

👍 TODAY'S TRIUMPHS

👎 TODAY'S CHALLENGES

💡 WHAT I LEARNED FROM TODAY:

🏆 MY TOP GOAL FOR TOMORROW:

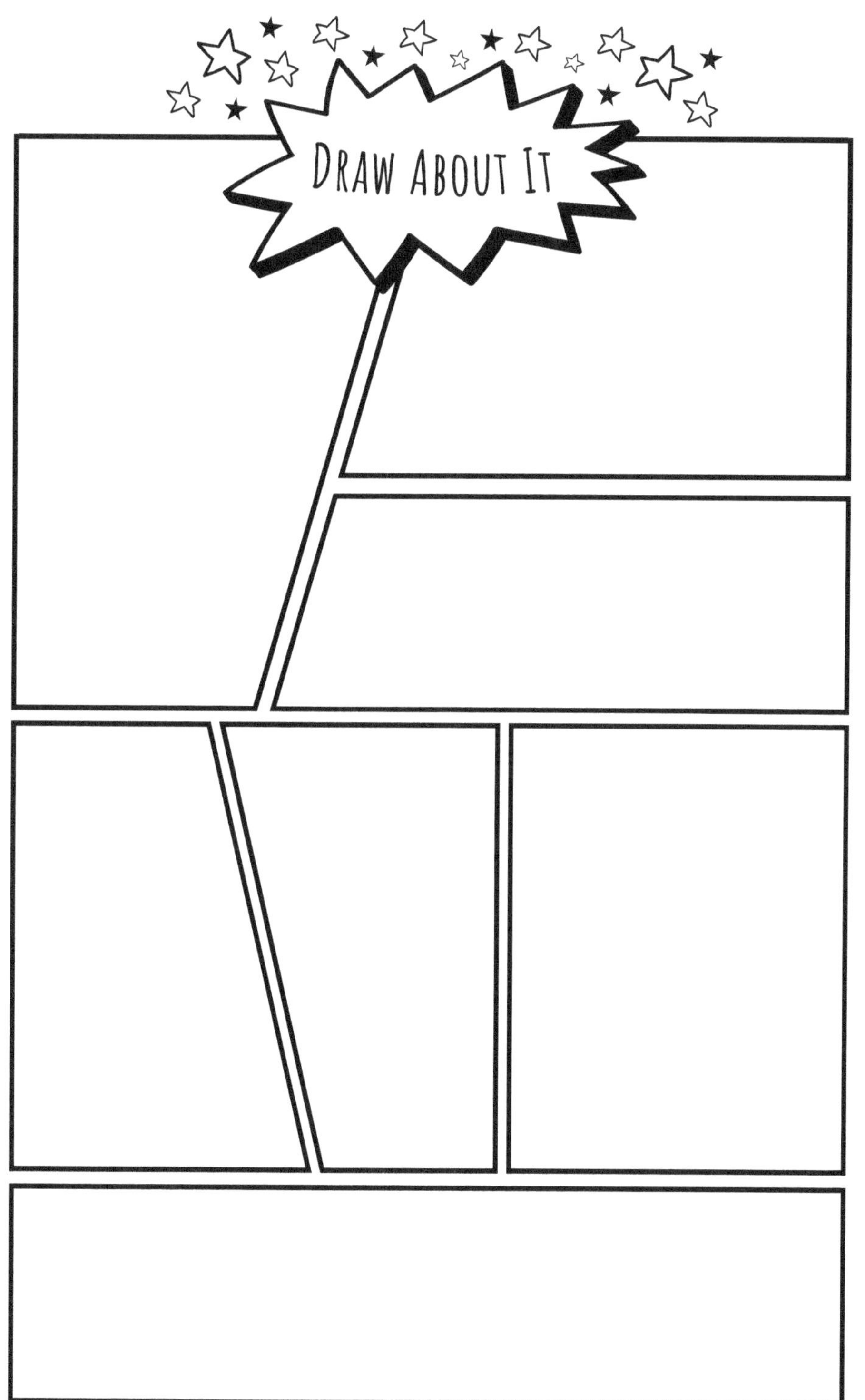
Draw About It

DATE: S M T W TH F S __ / __ / __

OVERALL TODAY WAS: ☆ ☆ ☆ ☆ ☆

👍 TODAY'S TRIUMPHS

____
____
____
____
____
____
____
____
____

👎 TODAY'S CHALLENGES

____
____
____
____
____
____
____
____
____

💡 WHAT I LEARNED FROM TODAY:

____
____

🏆 MY TOP GOAL FOR TOMORROW:

____

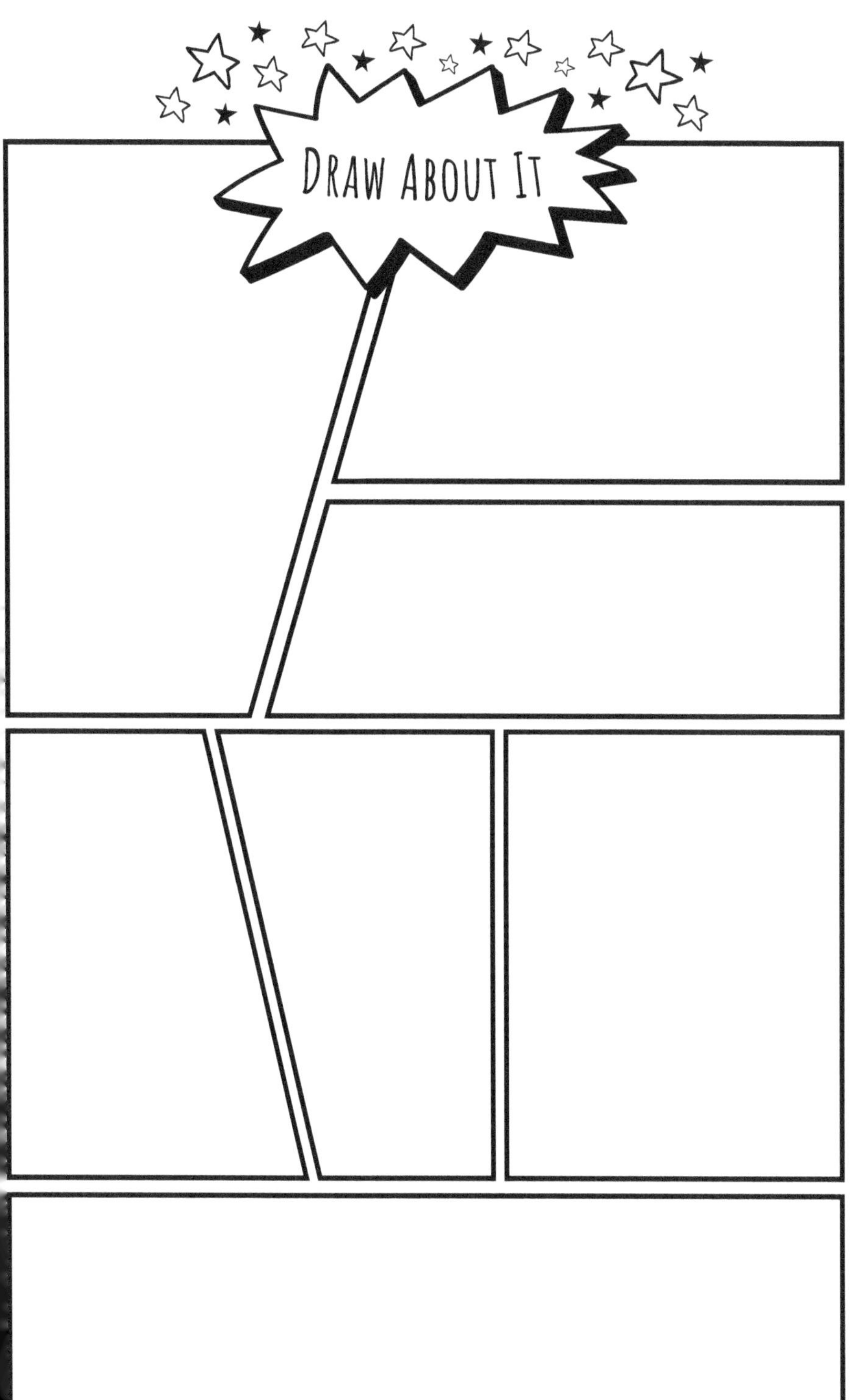
Draw About It

DATE: S   M   T   W   TH   F   S   __ / __ / __

OVERALL TODAY WAS: ☆ ☆ ☆ ☆ ☆

👍 TODAY'S TRIUMPHS

____
____
____
____
____
____
____
____
____

👎 TODAY'S CHALLENGES

____
____
____
____
____
____
____

💡 WHAT I LEARNED FROM TODAY:

____
____

🏆 MY TOP GOAL FOR TOMORROW:

____

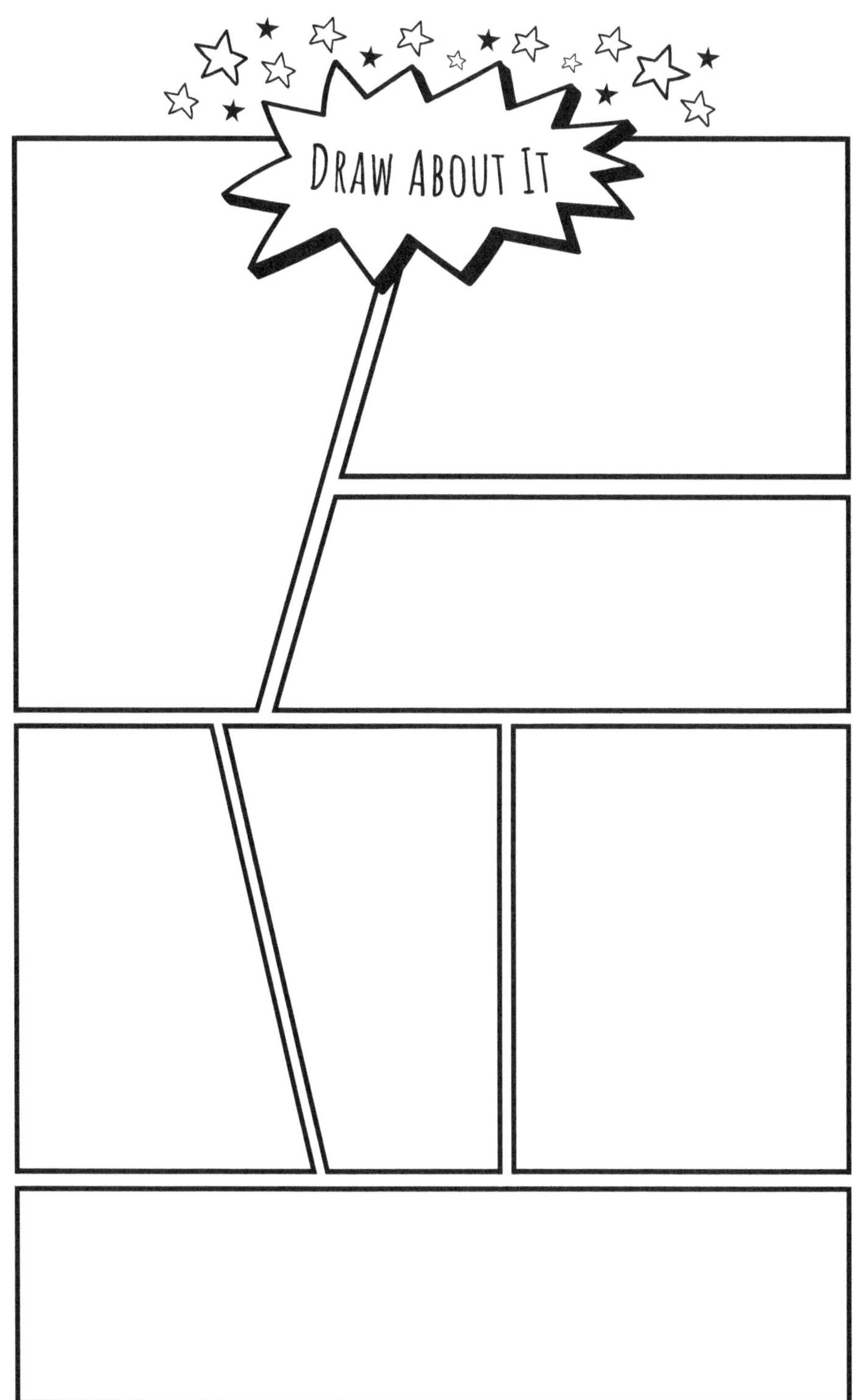
Draw About It

DATE: S M T W TH F S __ / __ / __

OVERALL TODAY WAS: ☆ ☆ ☆ ☆ ☆

👍 TODAY'S TRIUMPHS

____

____

____

____

____

____

____

____

____

👎 TODAY'S CHALLENGES

____

____

____

____

____

____

____

____

💡 WHAT I LEARNED FROM TODAY:

____

____

🏆 MY TOP GOAL FOR TOMORROW:

____

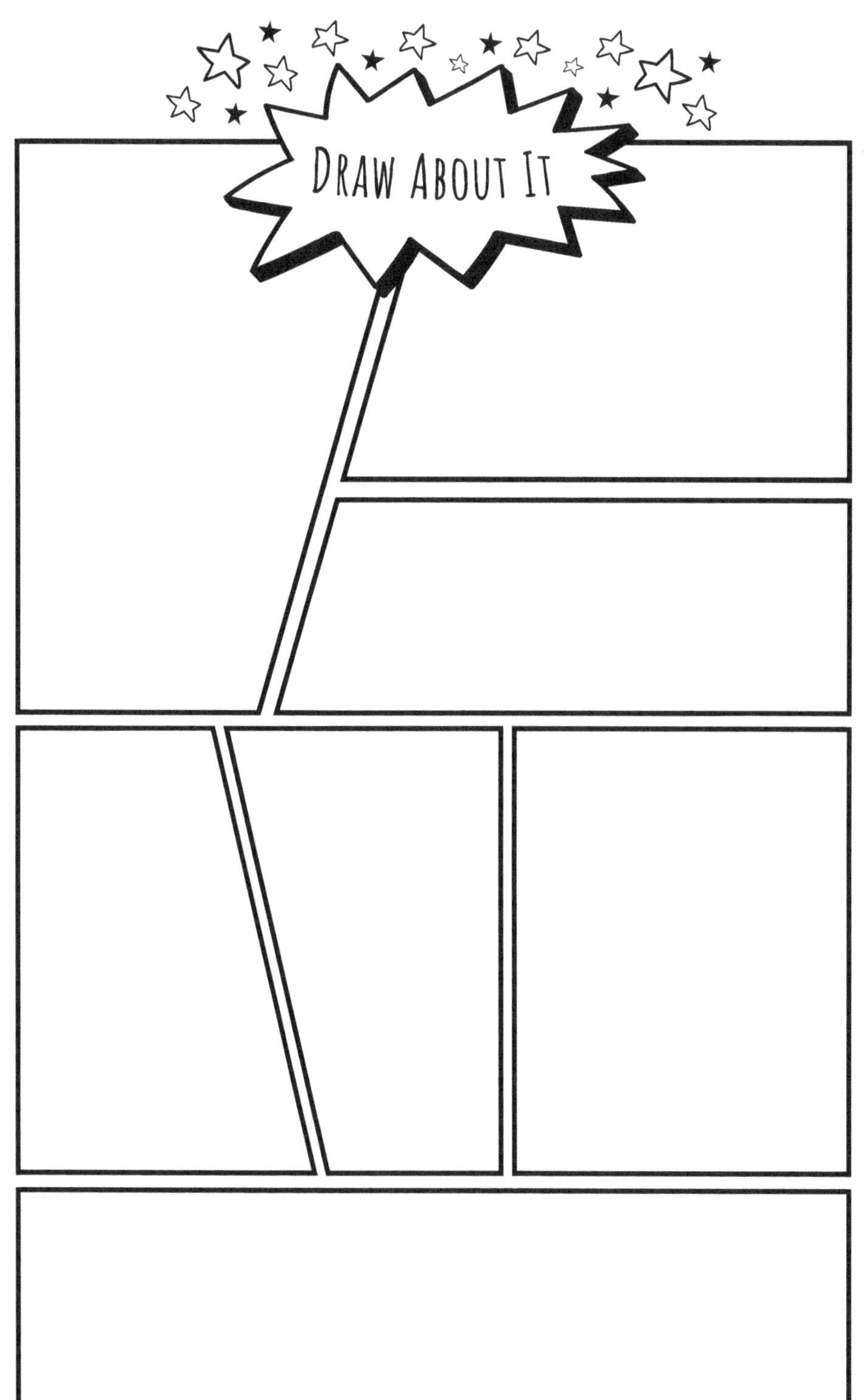
Draw About It

DATE: S M T W TH F S __ / __ / __

OVERALL TODAY WAS: ☆ ☆ ☆ ☆ ☆

👍 TODAY'S TRIUMPHS

👎 TODAY'S CHALLENGES

💡 WHAT I LEARNED FROM TODAY:

🏆 MY TOP GOAL FOR TOMORROW:

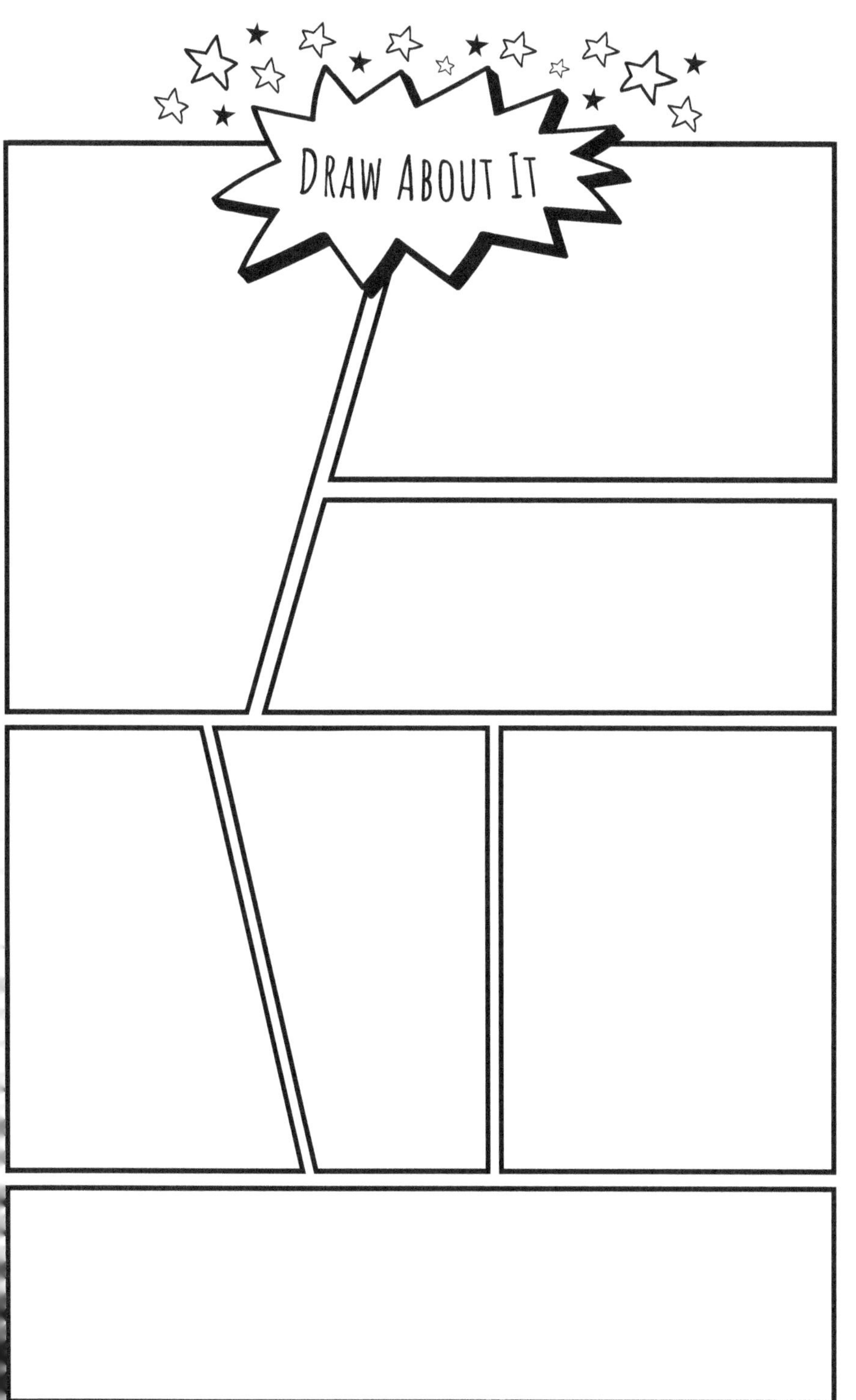
Draw About It

DATE: S M T W TH F S   __ / __ / __

OVERALL TODAY WAS: ☆ ☆ ☆ ☆ ☆

👍 TODAY'S TRIUMPHS

👎 TODAY'S CHALLENGES

💡 WHAT I LEARNED FROM TODAY:

🏆 MY TOP GOAL FOR TOMORROW:

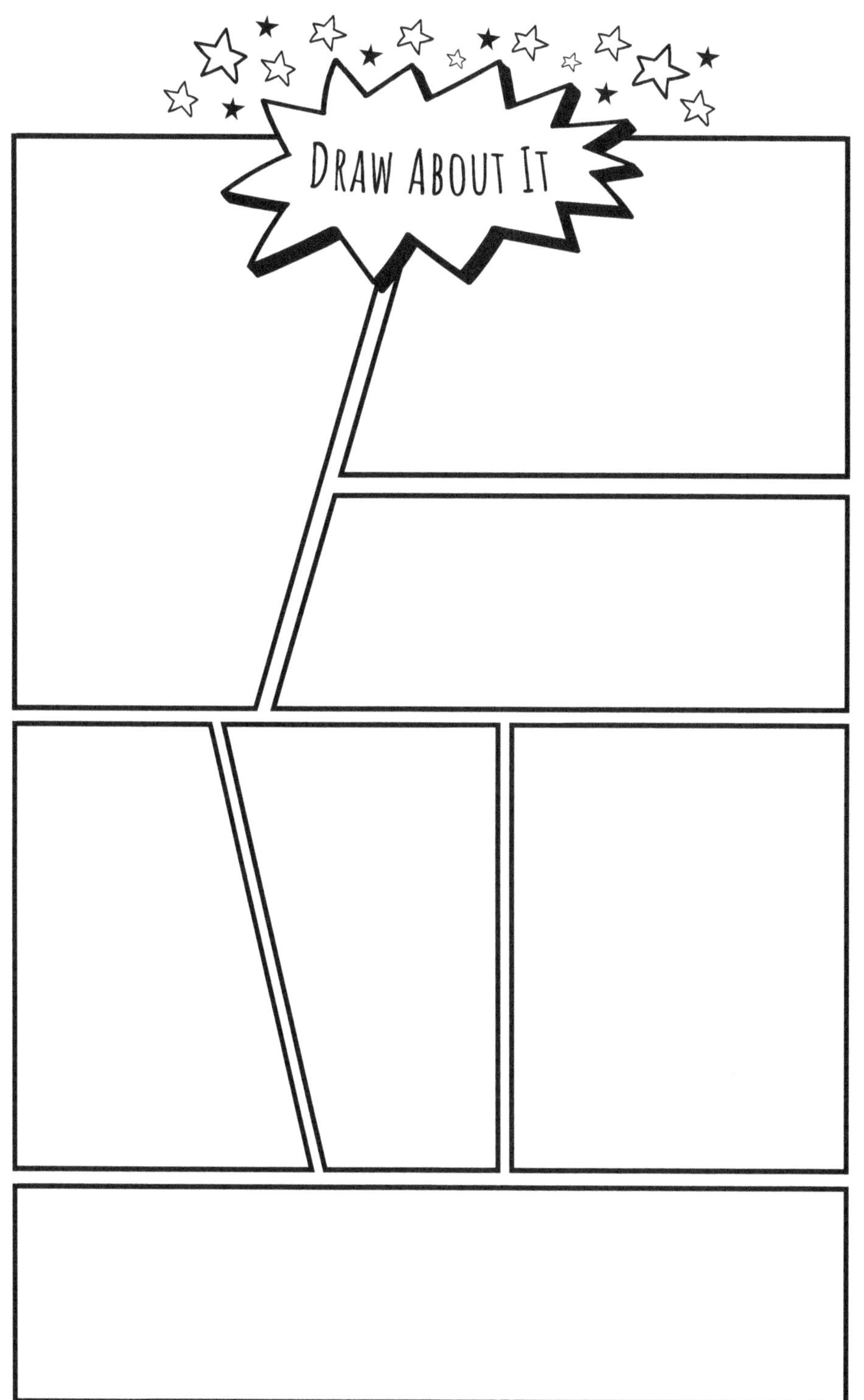
DRAW ABOUT IT

DATE: S M T W TH F S __ / __ / __

OVERALL TODAY WAS: ☆ ☆ ☆ ☆ ☆

👍 TODAY'S TRIUMPHS

👎 TODAY'S CHALLENGES

💡 WHAT I LEARNED FROM TODAY:

🏆 MY TOP GOAL FOR TOMORROW:

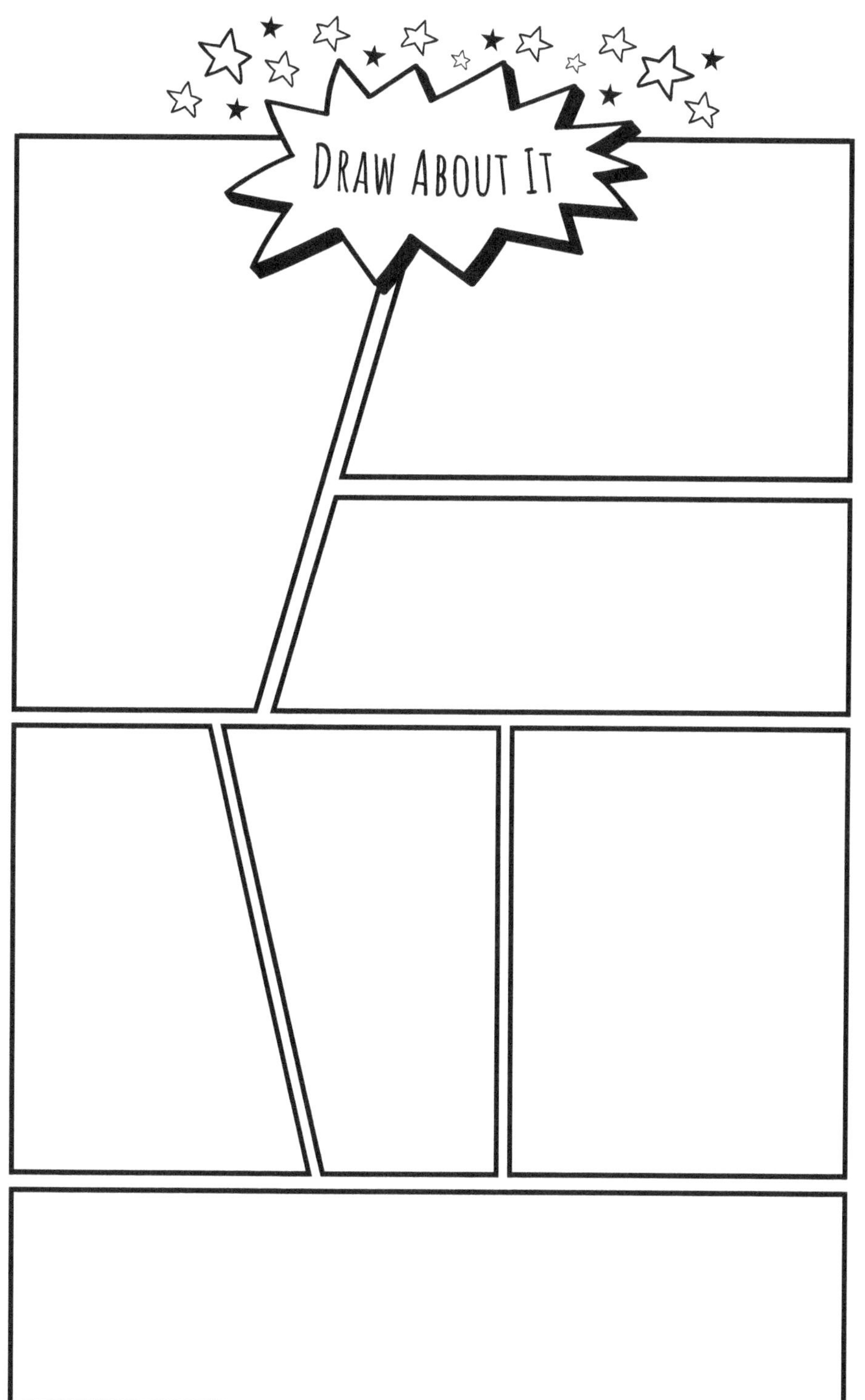

Draw About It

DATE: S M T W TH F S __/__/__

OVERALL TODAY WAS: ☆ ☆ ☆ ☆ ☆

👍 TODAY'S TRIUMPHS

👎 TODAY'S CHALLENGES

💡 WHAT I LEARNED FROM TODAY:

🏆 MY TOP GOAL FOR TOMORROW:

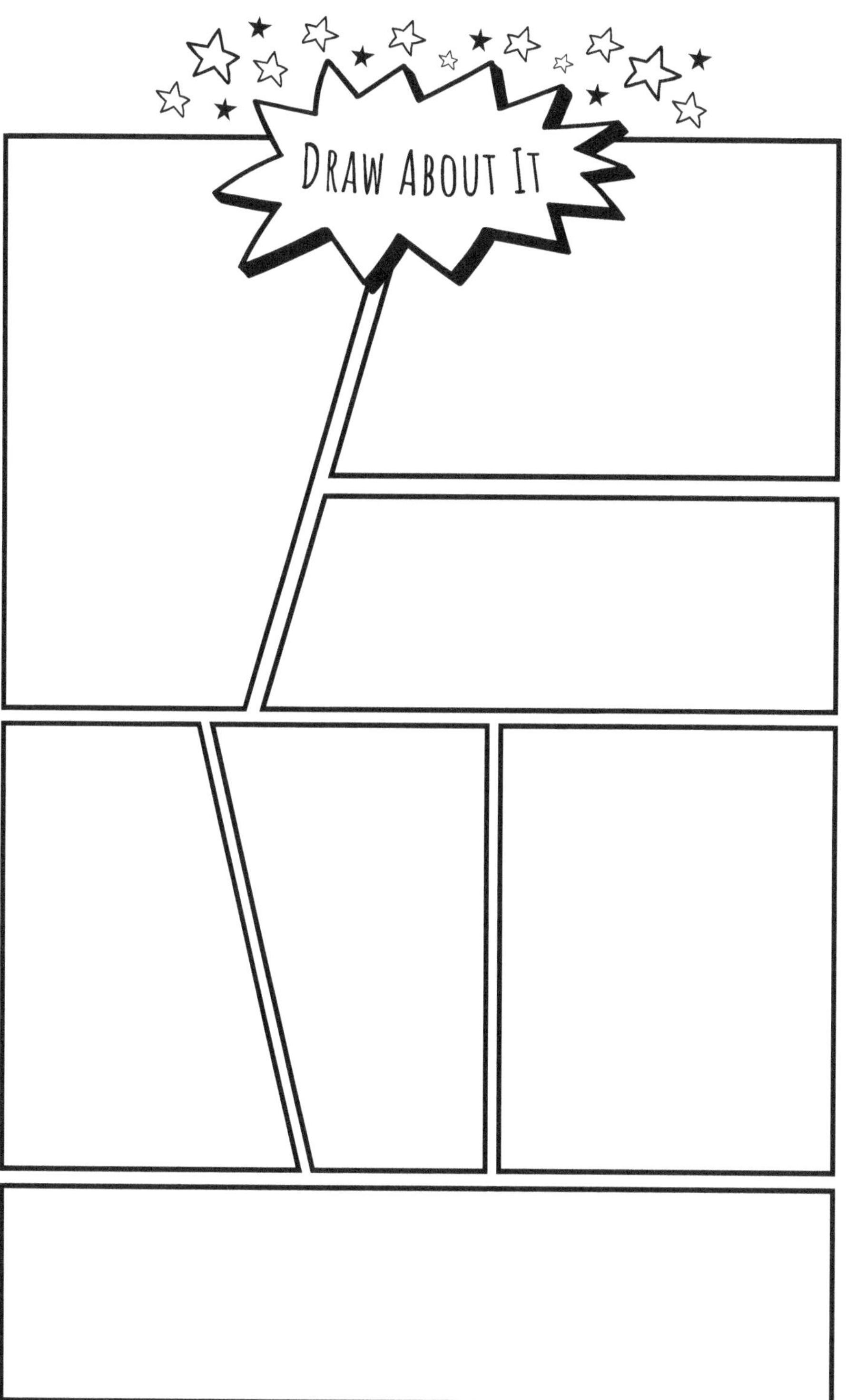

Draw About It

DATE: S M T W TH F S __ / __ / __

OVERALL TODAY WAS: ☆ ☆ ☆ ☆ ☆

👍 TODAY'S TRIUMPHS

👎 TODAY'S CHALLENGES

💡 WHAT I LEARNED FROM TODAY:

🏆 MY TOP GOAL FOR TOMORROW:

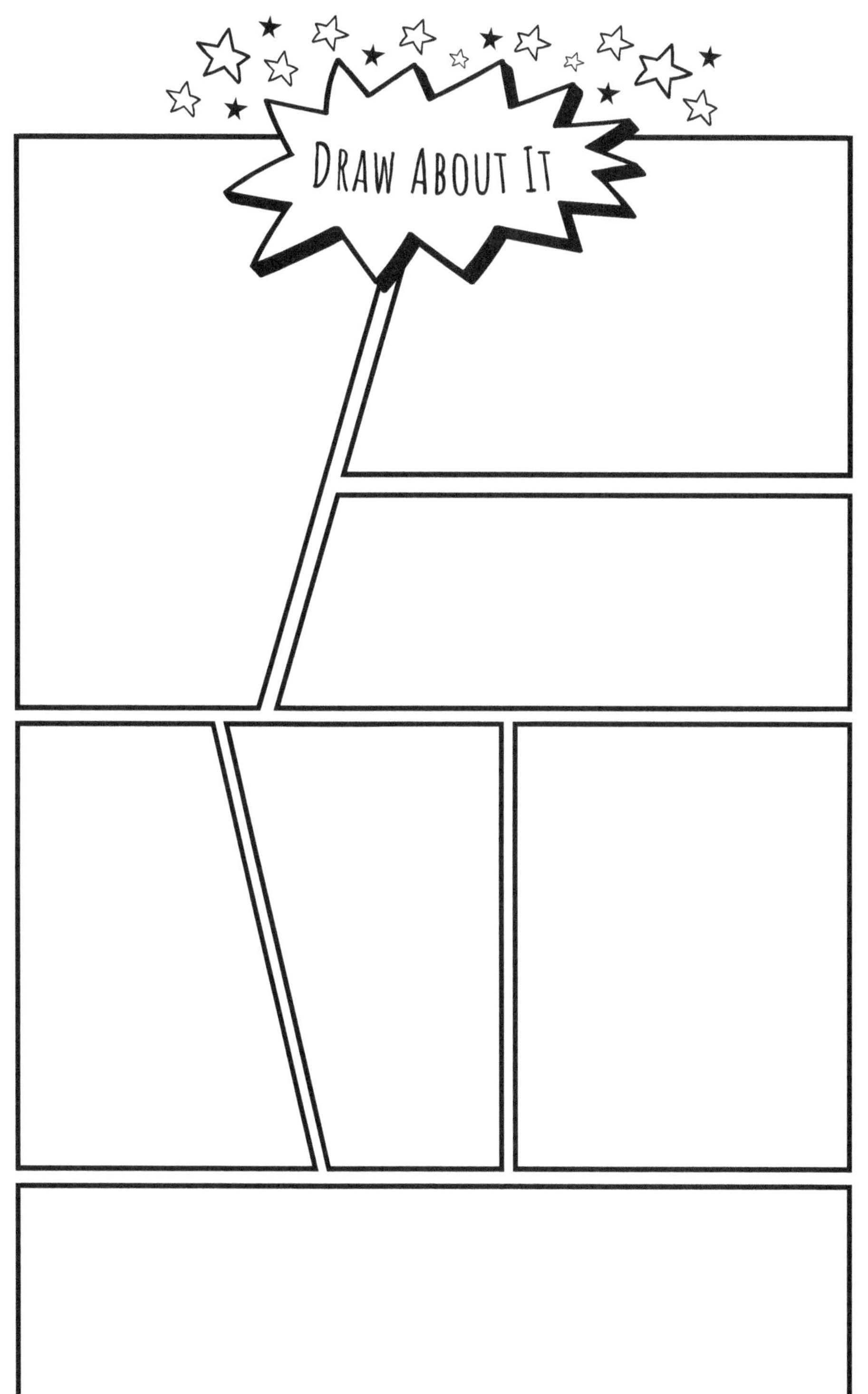
DRAW ABOUT IT

DATE: S M T W TH F S   __ / __ / __

OVERALL TODAY WAS: ☆ ☆ ☆ ☆ ☆

👍 TODAY'S TRIUMPHS

👎 TODAY'S CHALLENGES

💡 WHAT I LEARNED FROM TODAY:

🏆 MY TOP GOAL FOR TOMORROW:

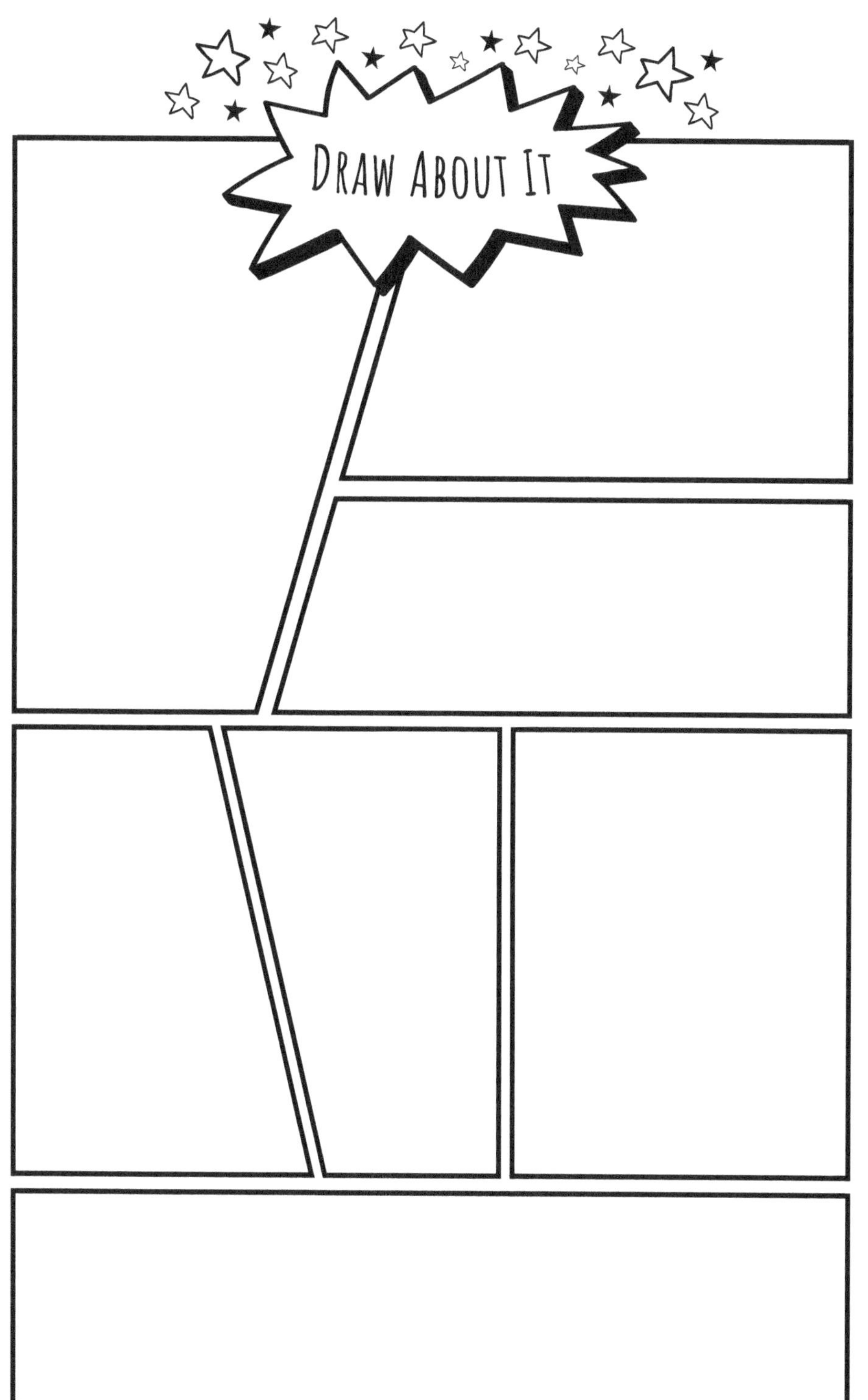
DRAW ABOUT IT

DATE: S M T W TH F S __/__/__

OVERALL TODAY WAS: ☆ ☆ ☆ ☆ ☆

👍 TODAY'S TRIUMPHS

👎 TODAY'S CHALLENGES

💡 WHAT I LEARNED FROM TODAY:

🏆 MY TOP GOAL FOR TOMORROW:

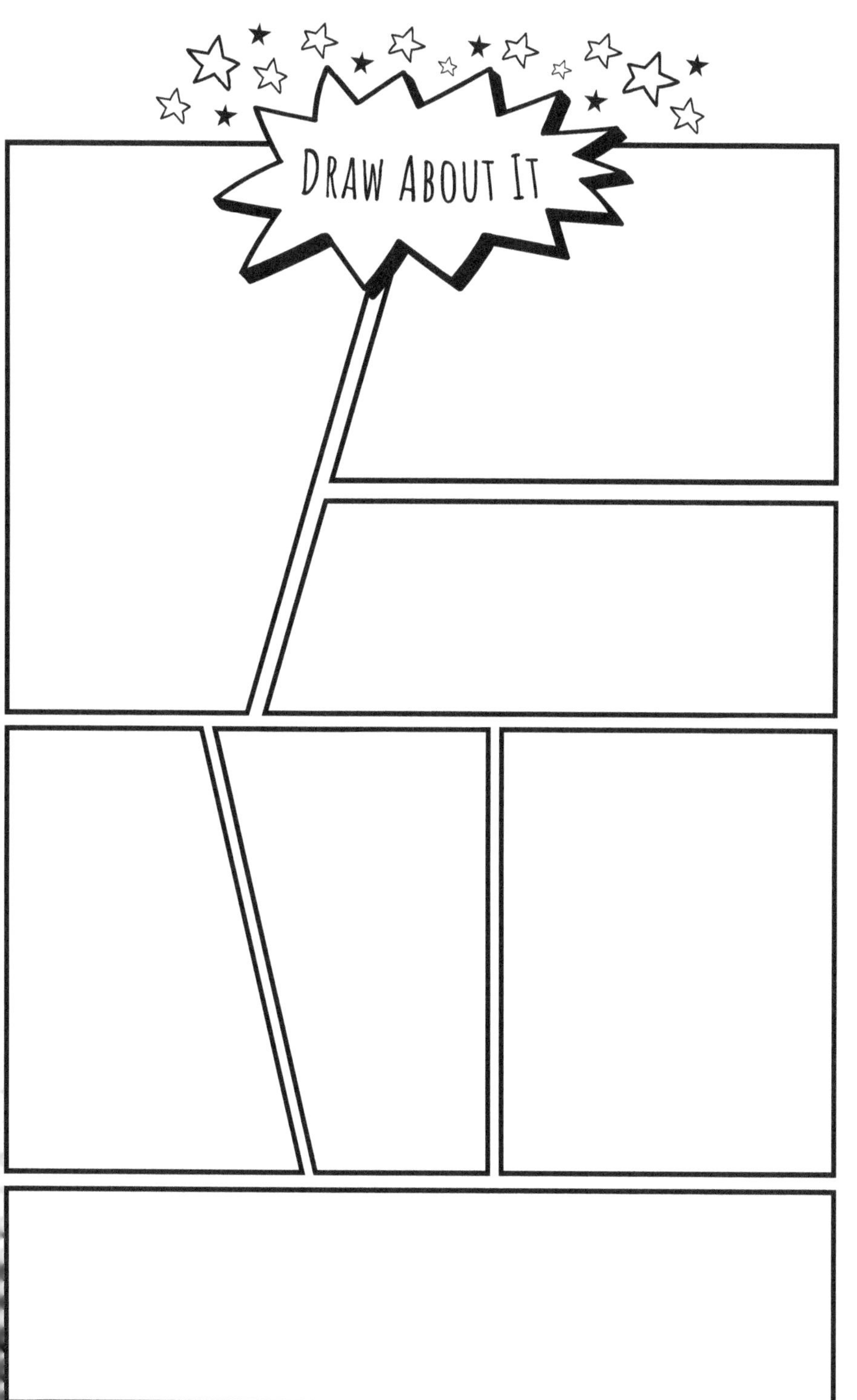
Draw About It

DATE: S M T W TH F S __/__/__

OVERALL TODAY WAS:

👍 TODAY'S TRIUMPHS

👎 TODAY'S CHALLENGES

💡 WHAT I LEARNED FROM TODAY:

🏆 MY TOP GOAL FOR TOMORROW:

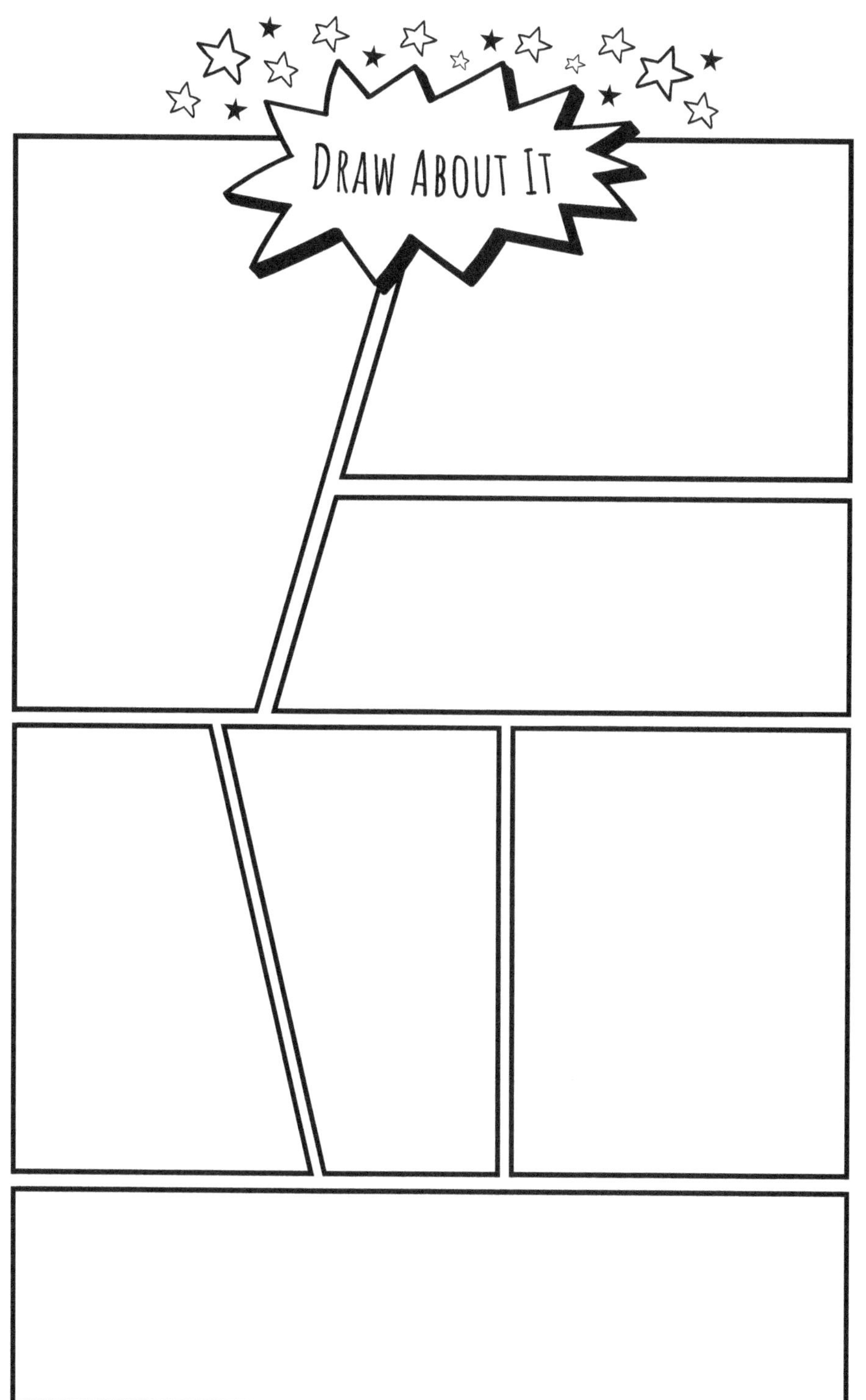
Draw About It

DATE: S M T W TH F S __ / __ / __

OVERALL TODAY WAS: ☆ ☆ ☆ ☆ ☆

👍 TODAY'S TRIUMPHS

👎 TODAY'S CHALLENGES

💡 WHAT I LEARNED FROM TODAY:

🏆 MY TOP GOAL FOR TOMORROW:

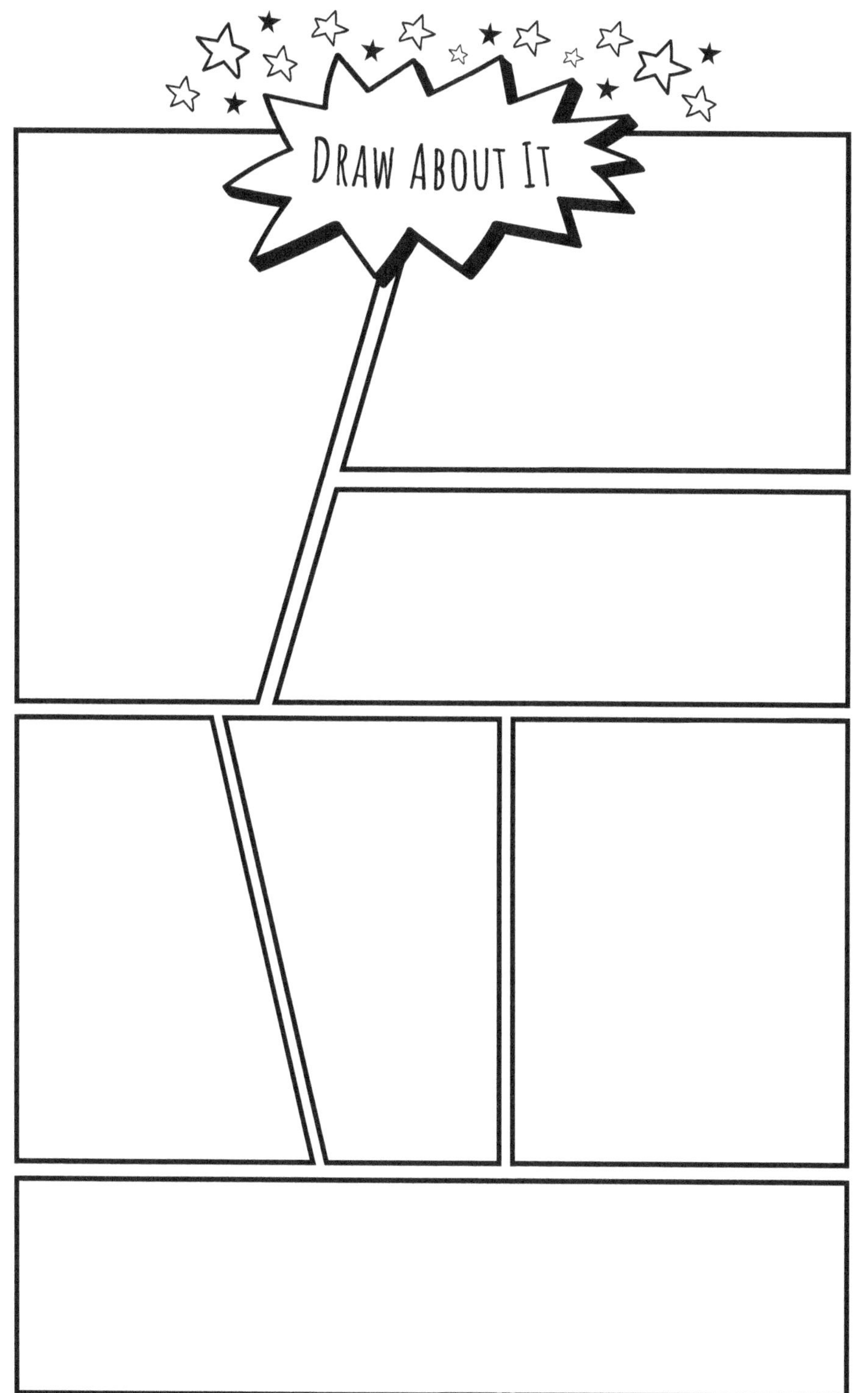

DRAW ABOUT IT